DEAR
EVERYONE

DEAR EVERYONE
MATT SHEARS

BROOKLYN ARTS PRESS | NEW YORK

Dear Everyone
© 2016 Matt Shears

ISBN-13: 978-1-936767-34-2

Cover Art: "Cloudscapes #11" by Raúl Lázaro. Cover & Interior Design by Martin Rock. Edited by Joe Pan.

Published in the United States of America by:
Brooklyn Arts Press
154 N 9th St #1
Brooklyn, NY 11249
WWW.BROOKLYNARTSPRESS.COM
INFO@BROOKLYNARTSPRESS.COM

Distributed to the trade by Small Press Distribution / SPD
www.spdbooks.org

Names: Shears, Matt, author.
Title: Dear everyone / by Matt Shears.
Description: New York : Brooklyn Arts Press, 2016.
Identifiers: LCCN 2014019658 | ISBN 9781936767342 (pbk. : alk. paper)
Classification: LCC PS3619.H4343 A6 2016 | DDC 811/.6--dc23
LC record available at https://lccn.loc.gov/2014019658

FIRST EDITION

CONTENTS

EMERGENCY
PROCEDURES

some filmic aggressions. Vengeance is

well played! Good Shepherd: come again?

again on welfare? I lost all feeling

in the extremities, the hardware. The engines

scrambled away. I crowd-sourced

destitute constructions, federal theater.

gametes, zygotes, genomes, DNA. Through

and throughout white flights, coteries

of Divine Love. My songbird unclenched—

Paraclete, stanch this gushing past. Provide

password protection, unsurpassable coordinates.

and as for the rest? Placebo or trauma?

Impersonals. Victimhood, drawn up

in corporations. Believe the rebrand

of fulfilled promises: the superhighway.

Stranger, self-selection delivers

iconoclasms. Remember: desire may

require backstage passes. Shareholders herald

the unbidden One. Lazarus punctured

thought balloons? Out stepped Persephone,

who complained to the local authorities.
Phlegethon lurched. Accounts Payable
received an uptick. For the self-interested,
xenophobes may disambiguate, impressing
purposeful radars. But who? Trend
squatters. The Golden Age of Reality TV
Re: site maps. Eyewitnesses are stranding by
but, in a sense, the right questions. Yes,
fertility gods reproduce dream, myth, sacrifice,
the ritual feast. Ophelia disinhibits, floridly.
O, oft revenged Paradise: whiteness. No,
rented cheerleaders may not be as peppy
or well-choreographed. The Golden Age
of Misuse, trending. Peep shows may provide
the basics. To understand what hunger *means*—
compost the forbidden fruit? When the rooster
dawns upon its gardener, kiss it all goodbye.
leave it to the professionals? Thus, masculinity
designs how the ingénues demur. Power raises
partisans at the air show. When optimized,

yes, the warrant, please. In fled time
regulators are forsworn. Catchall ingredients
and virgins. Before Mythos leveled
with me, Poseidon over-prepared
for The Ultrification. See all available apps.
To initiate the migratory impulse, contain
instinctual desire. Pharmaceuticals may answer,
see? The establishment of market protocol
curtails diffractions. Nestlings rooted,
a damnable scourge! A rock is a rock
to me. When courage fails: attack!
Opulence is a beautiful wish
out on the killing field. Gasmasks blink
in the hivemind. The neverwild buzzing
with recent activities. See also: Diomedes
and Steve. Why exploration produces
extermination. Every whale is a whale
of a shockwave. Attune history, whack
performability malignant. A trident, yes?
Bless these natives their reification

so sticky! Yuck! Impossible weather

my perjured swan. Then, Leda complained

to broadband subjectivities. May the best man—

survive the rain delay? Well, cotton candy,

hot pretzels, off-key singing: drunken revelry?

for God: so loved the world, He gave His dream

of omniscience. Frisk me? Yes, please.

in nature; but who killed the narrator? Props

to the messenger? To be frank, conversion

of some A-list stars. Flesh is an extension

of an idea I had. Beleaguered,

I doused phantasies. The class warfare

of online shopping. Makeshift schematics

full of the best intentions. The abject

eschew sympathy. Her uniform, so earthy,

buried the evening. Those punks

flashed enmity. The pilot wobbled out beyond

his comfort zone. Among the bons vivants,

we challenged the call. Sacrificial images remained

in the irregulated self, distended, breached

effects may persist longer than
banishment. Deliver a populist preamble
or The Law. When speaking in tongues,
the cardiogram may issue a total recall.
Is this love? Ceremonial burning? Well,
what regime? Hark! Who goes there?
monstrous animations. Arise Superhero!
Dos: for shifting windows. My lyre!
a decidedly unmystic twilight. Don'ts:
When I remembered myself
choking on daily tragedies, those
condemned to silence. Of mourning,
survivalists may inaugurate a Golden Age
to pray upon them. In the missive,
Form + Functionality = Dancers pass by
the electromagnetic spectrum, repulsing
unreal airwaves. In radiant flights,
a heavenly restructuring. Classifying
whiteness in the anxious, twitchy news.
Shadows lurk in the encrypted files

outside Forthright City: drop cloths.
We profiled civility engineers,
trending assimilations. Distrust excursions
beyond the accepted limits. Experience
bungles more courageous affiliations, but
yes, submit improvement plans. Benefactors
hustle operant mechanisms. The cell?
A domino effect. Thrill seekers
need not apply conditioner. Kill
your friends close, kill your enemies
abominably, publicly. Reprocessing plans
may starve your famine? On your word
or out at the Old School. Should the ukulele,
when plucked, spray flowers? Conscience
doses up. What quantum remakes the chorus?
as quotidian night flutters away. Anything goes
for another brandy. In the case of the missing
foreigner? The loss of personal space
highlighted drastic action. A bald-faced
fault-line. And corruption. Because of you

hurtling superfluid particles. The stamina
of the wise. Perchance to stream
faulty parts. When the mismanagement
specializes in cultural imprints,
always repurpose. Orchids, too, open
into some kind of bloody cross. Yes,
expressers, system flunkies, expel
all agents on the grounds
of euphoria. Livery switching, blanketing
grace. Fuel injection, jet propulsion,
planetary debris. Marine snow, some urgent
letters requested. A participatory
encounter? In the Imaginary
folders and folders of re-vision,
there are many stages of plastic-making
and fame. Of impropriety, the flashing
ID badge. Aha! Another myth!
Leopoldville, Stanleyville, Rhodesia, Livingstone
Falls. Where flak crystals the terrain, terror
firms resolutions, agreed? Romance

is derivative. As always, we cushioned
separateness and burned up together.
the current flecks, simply. A clot
may appear on the boulevard; occupied,
impending. Animosity garbles
in fancy pens. Yes, hegemony
cancelled coordinates! Disabuse them? If only
untraceable soundings mingled amicably,
lifting the baby, bouncing, into sunlight,
the inner sanctum, the sacred: OM
On Wednesday, _____.
Then cancel it, OK? Dear Everyone:
who will take the fall for the sloppy logician?
Circumambulation, genuflecting, and veneration
may require some heavy lifting.
As decreed: the stakes of the Imago
include dominance. Power fantasies ease
the limitless Beyond. And then some
antiquarians always remain. Share the world,
the well-worn sofa, the mass grave

answers passed on. Sub-primed movers
resurfacing. I selected the monopoly.
In my short shrift, I danced. I asked that
we christen a receptacle of damages,
misplaced curatorial feelings, emotions I
friended. Whispers tasered the emojis
into dust. For now: Andromeda may
require some adulation! Insolence blings up
indivisible factions, with libations and
sky-high rent. O, this penthouse
between us. Yes, it is always like this
in the house of non-being. Boo.
Attn: The Emperor of the Slums:
Clio dreams archaic curiosities. A sheath
for egg sacs, nuclei. You may remake your life
with bread and wine, or simply imagine
Hephaestus hammering the wind into crystal.
A parallel trek: my past, descending
suns. What have I constructed? The merger
of the waters? The docutrauma?

you are the Detective? In that case

it *was* pre-ordered. Now, we must sort out

The Beginning. When cornered,

capital fragments. Another wistful

magic lantern. Fffffft. Epiphany seeking =

a high traffic arena. You choose

your own shoes, your own identities,

destroying the cancerous bodies that fill

chalky desertions. Yes, commandos

may have believable accents. Masks

contain incomers. Boomerangs. Speaking of

a permanent fix, and destitution! The overpass,

when channeled. Revivalist shock therapy

knows how to inspire! What methodology

and the serial rapist, too, aimlessly surfing

boredom is the new integrity. I mean it:

no, to *your* health! Operatic but insolvent

To raise a hero or two, plumb the depths,

depending on the Phoenix. As ever, outsource

the marginalized. The figures shall rise

more anthems! The Surgeon General

incorporates indifference. Daisies bloom

forensics: still lives and the like;

midrange weaponry, a soliloquy

for Freedom Fighters. The greatest love—

O, that wicked, wicked fairy! The winged

chalk outline. Were I but a shadow

all express lanes must end. Yes,

upon this rock. Or this one? The here

and now? Pursue elegance, if you must.

how the logarithm sampled? Empire

the new imperative? Believe the worldly,

the instant replay, the greatest hits,

the video montage, the shareholder meeting,

the smiles of the well-heeled, the valiant.

Not what you think? Specialization intensifies

but the name really means _____.

OK?

It says here that the indentured servant—

And now for the good news:

beetles, spiders, walking sticks, nits
midges, centipedes, millipedes, silverfish—
My pills! My pills! Dear Everyone:
believe the statisticians. And Afghanistan,
Syria: coded indemnities. The pencil-thin
operations systems management is absolutely
a kind of trickery? Smash-mouth
indifference, metadata. The graphic tell-all
dropped some names. When insider trading,
visit a pogrom? And then more pogroms?
I will not flagellate myself.
I will not flagellate myself.
I will not flagellate myself
by God. Seven more years upon
the tundra, the arctic fox, the polar bear,
the permafrost, the emperor penguin.
Might perseveres. Rate happiness? How
upheavals desire basins. A watershed
of permissible behaviors? But not that
omnivore. Please cancel the advent

Dear Everyone: To encrypt
a common language, seek their whereabouts.
hash tag: totem linkage. The Earth Tree,
the vaulted heavens, the primeval ocean,
expel all foreigners? Poor Pluto.
Vicodin? Maker's Mark? It's no wonder
you flesh out arguments. Where specialists
enter programmable destinies, you die
forever and ever and ever. The insurance
of refined dreams. There is no 'you'
twirling the lariat, in a bandana, playing
to your strong suit. Look impressive.
excessive whiteness may produce chafing?
Afterward, the industrialist founded a ghost town,
notwithstanding The Average American,
interlopers, ethnic enclaves. A melting plot
has fewer answers than heroism, blunt force
or the Mighty Warrior Itinerary. Why
manufacture the death drive? Yes,
a pretty healthy baby, but in this dream
I will not flagellate myself.

I will not flagellate myself

with the magic of Hollywood. *Before*

the freight truck? I don't know,

maybe out in the garage? Wonderstruck

laws, sounded alarms. The Titans

questioned primogeniture. Engines trawling

through the slush of saturated images,

bridges to golf. Fjord! Yes, sleepy as

an oil platform. And primordial forests

blog about it then. It's your life

as well as Venezuela, Colombia, Chile,

Uruguay, Ecuador, Brazil. Prime movies

flickered exclusions. Find yourself

or become a cult-monster, oversized

or an ultra-thin phantasm. Reflections twin,

valuation may stream. Exterminations are effective

as in a *chemical* mutation! Duh. To prostrate

healthy happy bouncing babies

upon the toppled populace. Stumped

speech curtails the impulses, the streets

bereave secularization. Follow the tracks
to amity. Or enmity. What scrawls out
across systems, fissures? Rounds and rounds
of the expression of force? Somewhere
amidst the betrayals: the bare necessities.
You gallop when you gallop, Cowboy.
Exit polls are extremely fashionable
as demonstrations of suffering. Winners
need not apply. Shirtless? Well,
I prefer *my* delivery boy. The Colossus
as garden gnome? The challenges
of orchestrated tactics? Your hand
is my grenade? Zinfandel and a nice gruyere?
The swans, the geese, the swans, the geese,
the swans, the geese—. Perhaps you'd
partition Texas? California? There is war
in fine-grained resolutions. Imaginary friends
are not to be trusted. And whistleblowers
need not apply. These are the mirror-images
they love. Anything for Deliverance

pleased to meet you, too. Dear Everyone:
sleep it off. Since the airplanes, control
towers, evacuation strategies, we proposed
the past! No, poetry never helps
with the dishes. I will not flagellate myself.
I will not flagellate myself
with catharses, a flat-dream I.V. The body
holds it right there. The police dream
of bouquets and bouquets. Peacefully?
whose child had seizures? So unfair!
then the radiator fizzed out, like soda. You
haven't updated? Who can know you
without your avatars? The amputation defines;
where the flesh-wound questions? Oversharers run on
to the beach! Argon, krypton, xenon, and radon
may produce nobility. The splendor and glory—
Now that everything has been documented,
childhood awaits. Where I negate
my own negation? No, I will not flagellate myself
or my citizenry. Yes, peace is complimentary

shot the albatross? WTF? Dear Everyone:

dressing for success is absolutely essential.

Think about Felix or Emilio or Steve

or Miranda or Clare or the other Clare!

Yes. It absolutely has to be Paris, or

client-centered protocol. When mood lighting

just doesn't do it justice. Barbarians

need not apply a tender touch. Yes,

provide the experts their solemnities,

or take the express bus to Wonderland?

A singing telegram? Really? Bluebloods

dressing down Tent City. No!

No! No! No! No! No! *Flashdance*

and trivia night. And Paris decided:

Helen, late of Sparta. Now then:

answers drink in eternal spring: humanity

is obsolete. The Other is obsolete.

I will not flagellate myself.

I will not flagellate myself

or my many many many friends

clone phishing? Not these days! Yes,

a particularly aggressive cancer. Unreal!

How vibrations return us to our primal

powers. I am an isolate pixel, blinking,

a broken speaker, scrambled frequently. Yes,

ferried across Venn diagrams. Nature abhors

a trending. The celestial fire of my cosmic

consciousness glows. Infrared portals:

like the fruit fly, twenty-four hours

and flit, flit, pfffffft! Evolutions

are symbolic simulations. Upticks. Yes,

if the rich and powerful consume

all family values, what about erotica?

Edible pajamas? Dildos indicate safe sex,

as well as vibrators, sex toys, BDSM, and possibly

role playing. Now that everything has been

documented, by habitual thinking,

selections are obsolete, desire is obsolete,

defections are obsolete, whiteness is economic

orgasm? To be engulfed by tongues of flame,

I left the philosopher, unsatisfied. Yes,
to reproduce the conditions, resulting in—
And there, lying in wait:
the next generation. Call me sometime
after the interpretation. The Beyond
left me on the halo side of the road. Bliss
requires instant gratification and free wireless.
A purple cow? Acrobats may answer
birdcalls, who knows? When talking turkey
or minotaur, beware the waxwings.
tongue-in-cheek, for example. Edison
answered the peasant tradition
with sparkle. The Golden Age of Spam
need not apply. Hot air balloons lift
hearts and minds. Fort Somewhere applied
to another final frontier? Adaptations of truth
cancel the wind, expunging the Divine.
Yes, call their bluff. The formulaic script
I cast out into the bubbling Demiurge.
Operators are expanding Time,

however. Indignant, we pass on

the annual report: doodles, squiggles,

curlicues. See also: Exhibit A:

oxygen-laden cells encounter the Will

of Will. And nature abhors

a battlefield. I come in peace, and

I will not flagellate myself—

Seriously? Options hedge, we plant

peonies *and* peons. The soil is rich

with our ancestral motif, backlit

with gratitude and wisdom! Physics

answers everything. Swiss chard, kale,

spinach, mustard greens, arugula even,

correctional facilities. Ambassadors

need not apply. Wardens need not apply

treatment. Which psychopomp speaks

in tongues? Imagine my coronation:

a bloody crown, and cardboard sign:

PLEASE HELP ME, I AM ONE OF YOU.

Things I remember: the last hurrah,

specialists are scanning the skies. Gray

scales don't lie. Librarians dream

another laissez faire. Properly speaking,

monitors fill the streets. Believe in

reptiles or amphibians? Nature shows

my sadness pressed, letters preserved,

the morning of the specimen. But dry rot

scratched animations. Pageants

admonish the bouncing baby? Yes,

operational logistics further docks,

insert bar codes in Shepheardes' Calenders.

Never believe the Neanderthal,

the cancelled ceremony of Deliverance.

Who knew Steve or Felix or Emilio or Clare

or the National Assembly? Athletes

need not apply. Conversion charts

need not apply. My lasso! My pistol!

Surfaces contradict me. I am not

not worried, but a little panicky.

Pleasantries and wish lists Do Not Mix

age old questions, but they answered!

Dear Everyone: merriment

is not my strong suit. Planetary debris,

the solar wind and marine snow. The fallout

is so complex. Consciousness

is always falsifying the data. But if

irony makes them happy... Why believe

these rumors of yourself? Blessedness

flails. Imagine that you are filling out

a mannequin. Whosoever delivers justice

is not my strong suit. The new working class

or a classic milkshake? Summer is easy

to break open, like a gourd, or a lie.

The crosshairs may cite history, while

the ground of Being always abates.

meaning that Steve knew, that Felix knew

and paratroopers need not apply. Over.

I shaded data science with secret feelings.

With who? For whom? Roger. Yes,

condition your responsibility. Goodbye,

red flags betray me. The leading authority

on the undocumented population, _____,

all domains name. A cautionary tale

Re: premature aging, the willies:

a monster perhaps? A bugaboo? Several species

of tracking device. The trouble with free

agency and escort services. Some vice

gripped my heart, and winter came

alive. The magic of the silver stream—

incidentals made me do it. I see

canaries or lovebirds? When battleships

sag in the rain. A moment similar to

believing in the present conditions.

Romulus or Remus? A total mismatch

prepared a nice spread for Friday night.

How my past disowned me. The present is

December, January, February, March—

When you pull on your carbon footprint

the phlegmatic, spleeny sort. Poetry is

OMG! Your boredom is so not unique

fill up my calendar? The bouncing baby

Aesthetics? Why the dramatic

flare? Records. They searched catalogs

in the atmosphere: chthonic wailings,

dependencies. The café remains

vitally important to the bourgeoisie.

a tributary evangel, some C-list movie star

killed the lights. The patients radiated.

The total number of satellites increases interest,

when inside the diorama, Clare, or the other

Clare...someone knew the formula. So,

is this a cut up? Poetry has so much

now that everything has been documented

for Steve or Felix or their spirit animal dream.

(Deer, waterfall.) Molecules are essential

on the Dark Night of the Soul. Whose imagination

drained power? Evacuation procedures

or Doomsday scenarios? My ancestors believed

in similar politicians, similar whodunits. No,

The Amnesty need not apply

salve. Dear Everyone: jouissance
contests authority. Throw a sparkler
at those turkey vultures? Imagine
an operation that is unequivocal
to the next operation; and that is how
babies are made. Posturing trumps
my strong suit. Perfect territories
elongate the spine. Your chakras
stir up the lonelies? When things turn
inward, watch out! Explicit directions
summoned her courage. Tracking devices
scoured the Twentieth Century. Looking
good! And wholesome, too. Whose cadaver?
The deliveries arrived. Shot messengers
need not apply. Community organizers
sanitize cultural formations. Control groups
articulate pandemonium, the logging
out of industrial slag. Greenness quashes.
Yes, emergency protocol has been established.
Cradle the bouncing baby, embrace love

but it cannot end with love? Not now

that everything has been documented?

Yes, but questions, like antelope, abound.

Everyone needs a theory, a one night stand—

When I experienced my moment of insight,

I said: conquest and remorse, but still

alive and kicking. Paycheck! The roots

install metal dictators. Warfare directors

need not apply. A garden hose sprays

the burglar alarm. Odysseus did, once,

in a celebration of cleverness. And women.

And wine. But the sea! The sea!

marine snow. In the Mariana Trench,

patents are pending. Extreme encounters

collected on video. I amass and disperse

what they all mean. Something will crystallize

the collective. To dissolve clotting,

effigies are impotent. Of course, everyone trolls

the galleries. How I yearned for sweetness,

the romance of the blossoming lotus

and the metaphysician. Occupations
demean the populace. Who specializes
in corrections? The transmigration
of grids, codes, algorithms, mapping.
The ladybug, the horsefly, the paper wasp.
Stock options support nuclear families
and space-age dreams. Believe the schedule
I have many many many friends. Thank you,
I am dead, at times a benevolent spirit,
at times, at loggerheads with these micro-
managers of alter-subjectivities. Compliments
aim to please. Under the watchful eye
of agribusiness. In the orange trees, the coyote
authorizes many new gospels. When
isn't the Minimart open? Dear Everyone:
consider the baleen whale, Leviathan:
phytoplankton are important, krill deliver
another oceanic sensibility? Really? Literalists
are endowed with surveillance. I preferred
your quest narrative, back in the day

so few answer the call. Shepherd!

Shepherd! Harvesting the salt

of the earth. To initiate new forms

of empire, para-consciousness maps

the outer regions: fervent rogue states

discover more algorithms. Please everyone

with kickbacks or schwag. Fire everyone

nightly. Sun-baked insurgents may

inspire the cheerleaders. Now

that everything has been documented:

other versions of America exist, in

heavenly peace. Believe the artists

placing unlikely bumper stickers, believe—

When the homepage codifies all history,

which amnesia will you prefer? Yes,

the signposts were all there, last I checked:

portents, omens, amulets, talismans. Yearly

checkups may prevent fear-mongering,

deleted scenes comprise me. I have fallen

away from their childhood. Viral memes

are integral to the equation? Wait,

something I wrote on my hand.

Ways to fill the emptiness: self-expression,

profiling, idolatry, guided mediation.

When disrupting the natural order,

always be nice. And Clare and the other

philosophical distinction. Scanning

old friends. Rerouting. The Furies

still inhabit these castles of the mighty.

Psst: the routine of upgrading syncs

insurance forms? Wild-eyed, unviable,

the victim begged: please, please don't

do this! Or this? It is easier to define situations

with product placement. Crime scenes

may indicate articulate mammals. Europeans

positioned subjectivities, categories

in excess, or degeneration. Paul Simon

burdens the future. Consider puffins

or barbecue tools; seek and destroy scenarios.

I effaced her online personality, but a lot

depends on the personal security industry

when the mailman delivers meaning itself,
public savants may disambiguate Google. Toggle
your own self-image. In the evening mists,
mushiness and romance. There is a video clip
of this: Tuscany or Languedoc, one
mountain or another. Something sacred. Yes,
the hijackers impressed the nation
in many ways: We managed to carry on?
No! We got engaged! I dredged allegiance,
distrust yourself, or contamination follows.
ordained online? Seriously? Dear Everyone:
yes, but not like Kurt Cobain
or some other pop culture martyr. See also:
the philosopher addressed in hypotheses.
Grenadine, Triple Sec, or Gray Goose? Well,
moving on to the final round. Followers
spill tradition. Restlessness builds deus ex machina.
For interpretations of absence, provide
distress signals. Each contains a remote eye
your chakras warmed? Your strength

because I said so. In the airport,

Steve, or Felix. Emilio? The cellphone

caught in her throat. The violence

of the systems we live in. Escapism

need not apply. Critical mass

need not apply. I survey myself and supervise

myself. The answer is never as purposeful

as flowerbeds. Watering holes demand

veneration and hierarchy. Cartoonists

passed the legislation. Discover how the Ark

disbanded. Or how Saturn distended.

I am a citizen of the otherworld, a brigand

for truth and justice. The confederation,

the burning rivers, the dead. Photographers

need not apply. Notwithstanding

lionization or hagiography? Yes,

to be honest, excommunication still

carts the damage around. Oxen may

prepare the ceremonies. A bouncing baby

Buddha. Sunlight is poetry, shining

but bring SPF 100 lotion and Fanta!

men of the dust, the journey to the Oversoul

because Nero = indemnity. Consider

a surprising rainbow! The countryside

blended nicely, but I panicked and

raised some eyebrows. Hegemony is

which story did she eat? Believers do so much

damage. Discover sensational getaways

I won't return to! Finite is finite. Chaos

means I will not flagellate myself

in public. The roadside altar, offerings

but we always loved the exercise!

Omniscience delivers knowhow. Patience

learns its script. Some may falter, kowtow;

the winged remain. More religious

admonishments. Any questions? I lost you

there on the thoroughfare. Would you

believe it? Semiotics said some terrible things,

statistically speaking. Anomalies reposition.

The janitor need not apply teleology

during the Golden Age. Fatherless

loci, silences. Re: _____,

one fantasy novel or another. Anyhow,

neon signs? In the manufacturing sector? Why

populate the wilderness? Yes, Dear

Everyone, the enforcement will be

short-suited. Was there something

fecund, correctible? Breaking the orbitals

if not my oeuvre, then whose? Actually

collecting this shit? Due to an excess

of thundering. Either Zeus or Poseidon

modifies the climate. Io complained

to the local authorities. The cerebral

vortex, the karmic wheelie, Romans

at cross purposes. Thus, Destiny withstands

urgent motives. Regenerations are pleasing,

then, a bloodcurdling scream! Throw the book

at underneath receivers. Pigeonholes

do all the work. Like servants

at the big kids' table. Conscience heaved

another refill? Seriously? Percentages raise
umbrellas in the wind. Scattered seed?
The aggressively naïve continue
to manage all expectations. Is
experimental poetry still happening
on weekends? When crowd surfing,
perfection is extrasensory, a dropped
call. Dear Everyone: capitalism
makes a religion of self-interest. Images
stress the importance of false impressions
heading south: snow birds, memory traces,
the correct version. Highlights follow
how the crow flies. When stargazers
find something to watch. Consider
surveillance satellites, a well-lit suburb,
buried magazines. Betrayals are not nice.
POW's need not apply. Business as useful
itinerary, but in terms of downsizing
beware the undertow. Follow the children
away from the Coliseum? Yes,

severed heads. Beyond imperialism,

the parade, circus, or festival. Rockets

are believable. Expect chemicals

to love you, or to love deadly cancers

and hordes of deformed lab rats. Make space

in your heart and mind. Outside the biosphere,

the Organization, the mole, the insider,

the informant, their hard drives. Who adjusts

the boundaries? Sunflowers idly turn

whenever the bouncing baby spits up

amber or its insects. Push-button

particular anxieties. Troubleshoot the picture

of us: weightless, drifting astronauts,

tender morsels. The tide returned

with the bouncing baby. We purchased

experimental poetry with reservations

and pleasantries. Out in the Imaginary,

now that everything has been documented,

one must live simply or by oceanic feelings?

The affluent may still bleed. Beat them

to the revolution of Will? Kill your darlings,

revive awestruck evangels. As for

the underlings: press them down

the sidewalk? Take them to the museum?

class-warfare by streaming. Biograms—

I encounter the flesh, myself, I

question salvation. Because of the glory,

incurring the wrath. Automakers are located

in Detroit, Pittsburgh, Cleveland, Akron.

Or take, for example, The Scramble for Africa.

Arguably, these scattered matrices provide

security with minimal cost to human life

but monoliths may signify revisions of freedom.

you are a sycophant? Yes, the connections

have been made. The Detective learned

more gotcha journalism! Consider

the divine spark of Poetry. Tech support

need not apply. You will never recover

yourself from the wreckage. Imagine

offering fetuses to the pantheon!

I said: I will not flagellate myself until

the stroke of midnight, the coach, the slipper,

and Steve and Felix, and the *correct* airport.

Soundtracks are substitutes for emotion.

I graft myself upon pleasantries. My heart

is a lion composed of steel girders? Where

did I modulate graphs, topographies? Stolidly, I

pressed into the sea of groupthink. You know what?

Everyone bleeds somewhat differently. Culture

was crushed by a centaur that reared! No!

And I said: not unless we have synthetic

warning labels! Some people! The past

did or did not do this? I can wait for, well,

for example, the search results. Informants

need not apply. Suicide bombers

need not apply poultices. Bystanders

need not investigate. Believe in psychology

and wonderment. These pills are for everyone.

Dear Everyone: I love you one and all.

Gunfire *presents*: it just does what it does

of guilt, remorse, etcetera: liquidation
burns a hole in the No Zone. Imagine
the bottlenose dolphin, or the porpoise? Oceans
may ratify false islands. One widget provides
optimum secrecy. Nothing requires cookies.
Remorse? But in the energy field, the grid
that Cassandra evened up. The wise
govern chicken houses with foxes. Anomie
has fun in winter, too. My whiter systems
clean the downtrodden with chemicals,
level automated statements; not to mention
cult leaders or managers. You may trust
Carly Simon or John Denver, perhaps,
or the FBI, the CIA, or the NSA. Who
requires special clearance? Social climbers,
I said: hovercraft *and* amphibious vehicle.
Remorse can be demonstrated by squealing,
bristling, shrieking, shuddering, or passing
out flyers. Cellular towers, erect men
of action. Who produces cycles of depression?
I will never stabilize. Curtail the id, I urge

special forces. And so the specialists
killed him, like a video game. Wherever I love
the narrative shifts. String theory impacts
the sociopolitical. Operators are standing
in the shallows. As for vacation hours:
verse can be morally fibrous, learning
the popular language may invigorate
where luxury awaits. And self-hatred is not
nice, but very clean. When will the population
eat vermin? Insects? What rattles
your catchphrase? "You can't win them all."
the cow, the field, the silo, the fence, the gate.
Updating is now 50-60% complete. Or,
notify the authorities. Greed can mean excising
redundancies. The upwardly mobile
feel no remorse. When bunk beds droop
or moods swing. Moles arrive in spansules
of truth. They slip into new phases,
you spoon with time. Abstractions! Imagine
bombing without answers or questions

said the ex-honorable one. So God says,

"Kill the first batch!" And Felix drops

his pants and OD's. Money is aesthetically

pleasing to meritocracies, oligarchies, cabals—

And I said: "Behold! This is witchery!"

called a 'plastron,' an exoskeletal

belief in poetry. I am embedded, paramilitary

postcolonial. Housing? Like a fraternity

only cheaper. Wine is navigational

and salamanders, newts, banana slugs

head for the hills! When aborigines complain,

invoke the dream of progress. See this

diagram of heaven? Take it and eat.

Remember Velcro? Teflon? How did they

condition the masses? Always check

the showers first. In erotica, sex is always

just a heartbeat away, like the cockroach

or death. Never, never, never, never, never

believe the astronomers or meteorologists.

Well, yes, I stripped out the engine

madness can't do everything. Sunlight?

Chlorophyll, I believe. Goodness

is in everyone? The human spirit

buries the hatchet everywhere

or in bravest Agamemnon. Depending on

the terms and conditions of Providence.

The Invisibles posed for photographers?

Wow! Buddy Holly or The Beatles?

Strike family values from the list! Why

repaint the vacation home? Fire answers

most questions. Arousal is uplifting

when fluctuations chart. Regulate dopamine

or express something questionable. No,

facilities managers need not apply.

I promise: I will not flagellate

the messenger pigeon? Extinction is

now? Three, two, one...blastoff! Consider

vaccinating for measles, mumps, rubella,

and smallpox. Life on the Oregon Trail

received a Facetime request: love all creatures

or die trying. When miracles deliver
the barn swallow, its blue flash, the country,
consider where waterfalls end! Yes,
they took off for Happy Hour. Anyway,
the wind sprint, testosterone pills. So,
status updates are lies, remorse
does as cathedrals do. They do, too. *Ave
Maria*. And furthermore, the intersection
killed the bouncing baby. Tragedies are—
Dear Everyone: network, socially,
business as perusal. The status quo
is redeemable? Check out this brochure
on purpose? Tarred and feathered? Drawn
and quartered? Deliver the precious gem
to princesses, kingdoms? Real or make believe?
Middle managers, leaflets, memos to the CEO?
Resonance? Manhunts deliver messages,
victims, the goods, or the 11 o'clock news,
Maryland, Massachusetts, Missouri, and Montana.
Jesus can be both tolerant and intolerant,

you know, *believe* the president? This reaction
is not worth it, Spectator. Falling markets,
chattel slavery, child pornography,
investment portfolios. *Extra! Extra!* Page 53
is passing you by. As advertised,
Will boys really be boys? Nurture provides
exceptions and a fine pedigree. Watch out
for diamondback rattlesnakes, scorpions,
intermittent signals, planetary debris.
The preview featured lots of explosions in
The Golden Age of Silicon. How new positions
become reachable: stretching. The new normal
may come between you and your values. Hmm.
"Metempsychosis," said the defendant. Yes,
savor interesting poems. Taste them. Yes,
poems aspire to the condition of music. Yes,
you should, too. Charisma is totally tax-sheltered;
still, perjury is sometimes necessary.
Limpets? Anemones? O, life is a tide pool!
Enjoy your catharsis, while it lasts

they missed the evacuation? Well,

good old-fashioned piss and vinegar

solves some things. Foreigners need not

collapse carnival tents. Bingo night

provides instructions for the excommunicated.

can't take a compliment? Insurance burns

fossil fuels; fighting in the streets. I said:

patchy fog in low lying regions. In other news,

the airport, the hotel, the bakery, the restaurant.

For shame! The military is producing

fetish objects? Overstimulation? Imagine

the scope of knowledge, classified information,

paranoia and mistaken identity! Theft

as mantra. Metaphor is important

at the Department of Homeland Security.

Excerpt monogamy. And Africa, Asia,

serialization, segmentation, the regime of

death is so uncompromising! Watch movies

in place of indoctrination. Where answers

need not apply the full treatment, kill

when there is nobody else to ask. Yes,
ideally, pack a suitcase. Grownups are
not nice, are completely out of touch,
but can be useful. He was not convicted:
let freedom ring false. The libertine
and the taxless society. Yikes! Believe
in the pursuit of happiness. Imagine Adderall
and Robinson Crusoe? The Swiss Family—
Nothing fits. Victims are easily
tortured, and maimed. The intelligentsia
sucks out the seeds and bam! Nature
is mainly wrong. Caribbean cruises
are rites of passage, and seashells, kites.
Consider the blue crab, nudibranchs. Imagine
refugees filling out all that paperwork!
in an emergency, love God. Believe in hygiene
when down on your luck. Go on, shoot
the messenger. And don't look back.
Then, Steve, and poor Felix and Emilio
Nothing is boring when fully mindful,

instead, assaulted someone? Reconsider
the possibilities. Beyond poetry
and energy drinks. The standard
looked flaky, a little misshapen. A bolus?
For this information to be public, wherever
they acculturate, words are coefficients of
desire and abject humiliation. Poetry
need not apply. When opportunism
reaches the summit, take a picture! Climb
beyond fairytales. The right publicist
may solve everything. When trying on
crisis management, key words,
disambiguate searchable friendships.
Marine snow? Phytoplankton? Angelfish?
totally unscrupulous! Because everything
has gone to sell. Hospice provides
catheters or bedpans, or both. Discover
the Golden Age of Hotel Management
or new ranges to contend with. Algorithms
of witchcraft. The Visigoths and Vandals
are registered as ministries of truth

when I clearly didn't ask! Dear Everyone:
question how subjectivity slacks off. Yes,
permissions blanket Washington. Courtesans
need not apply. There is always
Kentucky, racehorses, roses, mint juleps,
fancy hats, and the parade! Careerism
buries the hatchet in the populace. So,
government and thievery. That is not
what the other Clare said, at The Reckoning.
was something long overdue. How remorse
manifests, or some cosmic flickering,
darkness matters. Anything can destroy
the return of the love story. Yes, taxonomy
is extremely useful. When remorse bites,
like a bedbug, or a flea; softness, redness, itching,
or blotching may occur. Don't buy.
Position the star map, call the fashion police,
believe in urgency, framing narratives,
cheating death and all victims. Never mind,
your dissertation is terribly boring

out on the campaign trial. They are ideas

of themselves; you, merely a coefficient.

Specialists made this dream come true.

someone buried in the backyard? Or a stray

shot. Violence is everywhere. Demonstrators

need not apply. Retail therapy, then,

buyer's remorse! Labradoodle or Dalmatian?

little girls like long hair, sparkles, and dresses

but can be so manipulative! To become a princess,

I said: Off the chairlift! Behold: the American

Bison beyond the sanctuary. My psychoses

love me. Self-reflexivity knows all:

the scripts, the actors; the alternate endings

burn up terrorists, and their families. More

effective than the police dream? Surveillance

asks questions later. Just then, the arrival

of nuclear warheads. Excuse me? Not that

truth is *not* necessary, but… Old rage

need not apply. Imagine the poorhouse,

the messenger widget. Ordinarily,

full of roughnecks. The muralist of
warblers, songbirds, assault rifles. Species
may rupture formatting. New relationships
satisfy cravings. What is American
poetry but interesting acceptance letters?
Doesn't sell. No one reads but everyone
texts. Not exactly the literary type, surely
ideologues need not apply. Life cycles
are liberating. And objective science
posited sexual relations? The sign said:
APPLAUSE. They buried the hatchet
in reporters. Now that the Middle East
is extremely popular. Damage control or
dimming the lights, cuing the background music.
With depression, genetics explains suffering
as ancient wisdom. Or how self-deception
may shape their avatars. Insert collagen
into imaginary lives. The specter of themselves
is everywhere. Dear Everyone:
I will not flagellate myself. I said:

it must end with love, or grisly death.
They'll believe anything! Consider
overlapping advertisements. The new you
is organized by systems management,
expressions of self-aggrandizement
and market research. Disown myself? Now
that everything has gone to tell all. Dear
Everyone: thank you for the memories
and talk therapy. To your battle stations!
Remember: everyone is unique.
Thank you for considering. Nostalgia grew
a pair. You or someone like you may locate
remorse out on the final frontier. Nationalism?
No, neither Steve nor Felix nor Emilio
nor Miranda nor Clare nor the other Clare.
Globalization just fell off the face of the map!
An imposition? A burning sensation? Déjà vu?
So & So's Greatest Hits? Venture capitalists
need not apply. Life coaches need not apply
the final solution. Thank you for calling

TOTAL QUALITY
MANAGEMENT
OR
ESSENTIALISM

difficulty is essential. Deliver
a priori understanding. Yes,
the shelves beyond the alphabet
squandered their ideas. Of home
and homeland. When opportunity
struck gold, the maintenance crew
erected violence. Towers of reason
swimming in vitro, in utero; indivisible.
Research is essential. To sanction
the body policy. Dramatic renderings
provided another important anecdote:
Sheldon or Randy, the medicine men,
the Masters. Ceremonial chieftains.
For antiquarians: a labor of love.
The extras were sent telescopes. Smile!
So this is earth? Well-spoken children
are believable. Yes, the labor force
loves ideologues. God is technology
but too old to understand it. So true.
I should have been a lawyer

winners aren't born extremely gifted,

but in profile, matchmakers may

spare. Stamina is essential. Provide values,

morals, ethics, and contraception. Imagine

the platypus! Because no one believes it,

factory workers? Everyone computes

differently. Research is everywhere. Well-

resourced procedure manuals are also available

for companions. The customer is always

blight? O, for someone to go to the lake with me!

Randy or Sheldon, the charismatic one.

Where idealism is essential, suppose

the cadaver, unfrozen, was spirited

away! Why culture-mongers threaten:

I should have been a consultant

and arrived completely wasted! The registry

dropped off the delinquents. Yes,

always yes. Problems are not unique;

consider horoscopes. Suppose the headless

mannequin protested? At the Old School,

better things to hate. Because bodies
are essential flickerings. When
the ever-ready contagion slipped
across the threshold: empty ranges, uptime
clouds, festival-goers. Should you, then,
belong to a club? Dear Everyone:
disgust is essential. Impatience is essential.
The covered wagons slunk away, slicked
in mildew. Dunno. Just some naked
street urchins? Yes, *virtual* servers. As for
Sheldon and Randy or Steve or Felix: a shadow
depositing the bodies in the desert? Sun
is essential. The melodramatic tenant
loaded his weapon. Yes, the time has come.
church can save a lot of pain. Pain is
wanting to kill everything. And He shall
provide some nice music. Is sadness the heart
of truth? I want to beat the clock, to see
the last disaster? Imagine the consequences
or don't. Believe in love, or have

a back-up plan. Living with wonderment
is suffering? On Saturday morning
for example, the exchange rate changes:
burning crosses, for now. Something
will develop, like muscles, or the elderly,
liminality, waste. Theories
do lots of good out in the community.
Forms of membership or leadership may
provide justification. Camouflage forgives
the executioner. Similarly, smiles
are refreshing, and surprisingly healthy.
change the light bulb? My sight has gone
partisan, my feelings terribly wrong.
Yes, what I know of them. Judging by
the content of the caricature. The poem—
Examinations are useful. When properly
addressed, she jumped! Later, the prince
mastered philosophy. Rumors are skin
tight. Beauty is essential. Art is
not instructive. Words may preserve you

if the package arrives in time? The situation

needed some counseling. Hence,

a time for radicalism. Behavior

reveals everything, or body language

may further the abuse. Committed

to pleasantries. And how do you do

it? Father, I have sinned. It all began

in the land of opportunity. STAND UP!

for victimization? And he said: Go back

to the drawing board! Or onward

to the matrix! And she said: He shall provide

an optimum experience. When the world

became outmoded, we turned back to the land

of Canaan. The precise conditions

of the homelessness pandemic are treatable

with manslaughter? I pray by expressions

of beauty. On the empty road, America

is essential. Characteristics include: cutlery,

china, or wine glasses. Without fail, massaging

the truth exteriorizes the primal trauma

significant details, more narrative,
and listen: the last decade
was a mistake, but I've changed
the drapes, the placemats, the bedspread—
Gestures are essential components
of secrecy. On New Year's Eve,
I cowered. Fear is a useful motivator;
operators are standing bylines. When
the police-dream returned, I hollered,
"Smile!" in the parking garage. Celebrities
sometimes smolder. When the smoke clears,
provide cartoon animals, some voiceover.
Elections are essential. Democracy
or free agency? Operations demand
ideal bodies? For shame! Agricultural runoff
is going green, if you can believe it! The yachts
just bobbed and bobbed and bobbed. Yes,
they curse the downtrodden. Arguably
the most symptomatic of human beings?
A little different, but we can't all be

distractions, stimuli for others.

coterminous? When reading the obits,

sometimes I answer them. The lonelies

may orchestrate flashes of anger. Purchase

power stokes the pleasure principle. Yes,

mirroring monitors. The reception

or the receptionist? Well said,

back in Ancient Greece. Then the Romans

and Samantha asked: Is this advertising?

Linking is essential. Liking is essential.

Fraud blusters. The eloquent

marble statues, or hysteria? Yes,

when in search of beauty, the last refuge

of terrorism. Reasons to kill: #1:

psychosomatic disturbance. Imagine

that you are a cursor, an asterisk, drifting

in a swimming pool, with champagne flutes!

Sometimes I answer them, the scapegoats.

how *true* the explosions feel? Yes,

sometime soon. Somewhere near you

#2. Pressure in the cabin, sweet release

or grapefruit, coffee, brioche, yogurt.

Hunh? So you're the asshole?

I mean: lists are absolutely useless!

not to the perfect criminal, at least!

To the airport! With prices that low,

well, fuck a duck! Idealism contains charm

and may provide research opportunities

or pop-up windows, or cupcakes with sprinkles.

Shepherd: deliver the flock. Locusts?

Devils? Plagues? Pressure in the cabin?

Never stake a baby. Never smoke a man.

beyond Costco, colossal warehouses

firm conviction. When on autopilot,

the status quo may resemble the features

of racism, or biblical mountains. No!

When did he die? After the war,

I will Wikipedia you. And History

cried in her arms. Fleshiest of Imagos,

I should have been an astronaut

or rodeo clown. Thankfully, we disagreed
about everything necessary. Pragmatism
makes life hard. The officious
imagine private islands. See also:
multiculturalism is essential. A life of purpose
clarifies outlines, and sketchy characters.
Because experimental poetry
is not useful, you carry your shadow
and squat in the hereafter? For instance:
life insurance, premiums, disaster insurance,
salesmen, actuarial science, projection models,
life expectancy and the healthcare industry.
As for #3: whether to kill terrorists
or propagandists? Imagine pilgrims in
magician's robes, the Holy Grail in a saddlebag,
and brothels, saloons, duels. Outside the airport,
everything trembles. I dream impossible formulae:
Romance is Beauty; Beauty is Essential;
where flesh meets sky: the Sublime. Where
superior design emphasizes functionality

life is beyond definition? Transcendence
arises from the onset of symptoms
and, to be honest, inconsolable despair. Yes,
use the monstrous alibi. Do not believe
in flunkies. The automatic walkway
is empowering. A teacup Chihuahua?
prepared the sacrifice? Well, #4:
collateral damage. The scaffolding,
the Firmament. Delightfully tawdry!
Critics demand satisfaction. Your purpose
emanates from 'Sankalpa. Spring produces
the cultural imaginary. Jameson is
essential for breeding. Exploration may present
some partial nudity. When teenagers
go camping, watch out! Believe in pelts, trappers,
massacres, and bathos. As for #5: the mad.
Now that everything has been documented
for Sheldon, or Randy, or Steve. Trust can be
damaging? Reputations are synthetic.
Love = Shanthi, Shanthi, Shanthi.

#6: murder, mayhem, and bloodshed.

A stray bullet, or intentionality? Blonde

can work. If the ceremony

demands an apology, forget it.

And he said: this pilot is fatigued.

And she said: this food is terrible.

Ordinarily, masturbation does the trick.

beyond imaginable! Ultrasonic

particles mean everything? Capacities

for destruction, and an aptitude for

self-immolation? Torture is effective

when dreams fill with recycling, beware.

Composting plants better products. Out there,

the murderers and the murderers of murderers

have instant access, too. As for God

or the space shuttle? Force-feed the lab rats

even if you don't dance! Yes, purifications

are essential; supposing first position

Since the onset of symptoms? I love

in the spirit of Pliny. Monoliths? Yes

different positions! Some truly senseless
compromises. Affects and defects:
the home, or the homeland? Wait until
the luminaries arrive. #7: emotion
can be painful. Surrender
is feckless. Since the onset of symptoms
and illusions. The matchless society
brandishing tire irons. Musicians
need not apply. Ideas fill out idioms.
LeBron James is essential. Playing
until the bacchanal! Sunsets are beautiful
since the onset of symptoms. No!
and flashed the librarian! What?!
knockwurst, cheddarwurst, or bratwurst?
Delivery optimization. Fertility markets
the concept album. When leopard-skin
prints irregular chemistries, then
polymaths enter the manifold. Yes,
The Democratic Republic of the Congo
and starlets, ingénues. A new princess

so you're the asshole? Well,

invertebrates once ruled. Consider

the Lernaean Hydra? The shot

messenger once believed in beauty,

as well. Culture is sick? Since the onset

of spontaneous overflows, my heart

cracked its spine. The horseshoe crab,

coral reefs, sea anemones, clownfish.

Ordinarily, I am the last of the line,

but as for #8: since the onset of symptoms—

Hosanna in the highest, rigor mortis,

and peristalsis. Connections

are essential. The opportunist slipped

inside the station, in the police-dream.

And he said: sport fishing!

And she said: leave the fauna

to Providence? The pounding surf

is beautiful. When permissive, poetry

is burgeoning aggression? No way.

Dear Everyone: the man of impulse

owns bucolic plantations, stock markets.

birds of paradise? Rather winsome

Disney characters. Is the reason for living

burning larva into my skin? And #9:

RPG's, going commando, careerism

is essential. When androids rule, bliss

parades naked women around? Yes,

in the court of nothingness: poetry

and lyres; ablutions, prayer and sacrifice.

Sexting? Is pornography apropos of

the yoga of poetry? The ecosystems

of unrequited desire. When considering

unicorns, dragons, fairies, wolves, doves,

sorcery, and sexuality. German fairy tales

insinuated it! Believe in the Savior, absolution,

ulterior motives. When clothing your Imaginary,

first, drop dead. The experts will arrive

to cart you away. Your proxy will deliver

all those enamored with brute force. White

skin is essential. Life everlasting proposes

better things to hate: tax shelters.

Whodunit? Even the gumshoe is dead!

beyond beautiful, exquisite even!

To the reservoir! Erasure happens

to everyone. And there you are. Which

do you prefer: natural disasters or fashion?

When suddenly, cracks appeared in the ice!

Like no way! And Katarina and Debi

and Midori and even Peggy and Sonja fall!

Whoops! Like hell! Exports dismantle.

O damsel: fear the lance, the joust,

and bigotry, too. Consider the sylph,

or Fairyland. Out on the reserve

generation, multi-factualism is endearing

and powder-dry, like a baby's butt.

I should have been a connoisseur

of online communities, the last bastions

or the skyway? In God's country,

believe in the fruit farm, the cattle ranch,

forthrightness, and the 2nd Amendment

because things live under the stairs,
problems abound. Now that everything
has been obliterated. Rebuilding can
be delicate. I listened to the voices
and look at me now! Knowhow
is essential. Consider the gadget
its proper cog, or sprocket, or circuit. No,
we are no longer friends. In Ancient
Athens, Sparta, Mycenae, Thermopylae—
Heroic spasms. Sleeping is difficult, when
everything either sparkles or unsparkles.
And #10: deathwishes, jammed
communications. Revenge fantasies
pass the time. Eliminate bankers;
strategic plans may curb your excitement.
And we are very excitable. Your hysteria
creates a new world! Is someone sleeping
the dream away? Incentives limn subjectivity.
Psychopath or sociopath? What love
recalled? Since the onset of symptoms

or Newtown, Connecticut, Columbine,

Colorado, Aurora, Colorado, Colorado Springs,

Colorado, Roseburg, Oregon, Charleston,

South Carolina, Fort Hood, Texas, Isla Vista,

California, Santa Monica, California, Washington,

D.C., Brookfield, Wisconsin, Oak Creek, Wisconsin,

Minneapolis, Minnesota, Oakland, California,

Seal Beach, California, Tucson, Arizona,

Manchester, Connecticut, Fort Hood, Texas,

Knoxville, Tennessee, Binghamton, New York,

DeKalb, Illinois, Omaha, Nebraska, Blacksburg,

Virginia, Salt Lake City, Utah, Nickel Mines,

Pennsylvania, Goleta, California, Red Lake

Indian Reservation, Minnesota, Tucson, Arizona,

Santee, California, Wakefield, Massachusetts,

Honolulu, Hawaii, Fort Worth, Texas, Atlanta,

Georgia, Jonesboro, Arkansas, Garden City,

New York, San Francisco, California, Olivehurst,

California, Iowa City, Iowa, Killeen, Texas,

Jacksonville, Florida, Stockton, California,

Edmond, Oklahoma, Orlando, Florida

or airbrushed? Revisionists believe in
poetry or opera is more outmoded?
Consider the life of the messenger pigeon,
for example. Since the onset of
the limits of consciousness
and its victims. When silence surrounds
the imageless factoid. Faith delivers
more water cooler talk. When insurgents
opt for the visionary impulse, the lifecycle
wails. Identify all searchable terms.
Robotics is essential; and laser beams,
special effects, sound systems, projection
models, CGI, and literalists. O damsel, destroy
the cutout princess, her burning dollhouse,
magnificent steed and empty-handed prince
with an apology. When French kissing,
open the mouths and allow the tongues to swirl
around the Darwinian fish. Oceanography
is essential. It seems that private investigators
are disrobing. Someone seen on video

and ALOHA! GREETINGS FROM HAWAII!

When sending postcards, wipe off

the bodily fluids! But jouissance

is essential. Yes? Dear Everyone: please

believe in single-celled organisms

when replicating. All history rests

in my pants? And the delivery

was right on time. Thanks be to God

and Jesus, and you, too, Holy Spirit. Whew!

What of the others? For this reason, #11:

hybridity, dissolution, loss of faith;

sloth, for example, wrath, even. Ideally,

this is a rebirth: simple folk. Yes, we gave

a passionate performance! Sexism

is bad. People are not always very nice.

I should have been a district attorney

or stripper of varnish. When medicated,

charming smiles deliver everything essential.

Where advertisements dare not travel,

the moroseness returned. Click on
the instant messenger. Persuasion
and witchery. With all respect to
archetypes, slabs of guitar rock
melted frustration into beauty. Living
is easy, with coordinates. Remember:
everything is backlogged. The chaotic
mercantile centers may require information.
Blistering? Yellow pus? I love
all the explorers! Imagine imperialism
speaking in thought balloons! And eating
from slop troughs! It pains me to say this:
#12 is indefinable. Rage is what it is.
See also: Menelaus. The singing poet
moderations of the image. Rhythm
is absolutely essential. Frankly, the radars
are ineffective. The filters are ineffective.
Imagine that all the armchair poetry
killed off the official story. Ordinarily,
a wrench in the machinery. Death squads

are not a priority! Since the onset

of maggots. Destroy your graven

dismissals, expropriations, urging

narcissism, and beauty. Poetry,

believe that raunchy game changer.

So he's the asshole? Yes,

Parmenides or Euclid? Instant

bulldozers of progress. Scantily clad

assault victims. Squeezing the cheeks

of a cyclist, maybe? Some files update

new diseases, expensive medications.

And he said: be specific.

And she said: alimony.

Ordinarily, I am nice, like people,

but hatred is intractable. Consider

the proper protocol? Listen: islands may

provide air bases, missile defense units,

cheap labor, and prisons. Nature is essential,

and knows its flowering shrubs. Cancer

or experimental treatment? Beauty

died like a dog. Forensics is absolute
because it's not you, it's me,
enshrined in a flaccid husk. The weevil
is but a breakdown away. Finally,
torture solves everything, like weather. Well,
armed guerrillas may provide cost-effective
solutions. Since the onset of symptoms,
I've arranged some keepsakes: red
begonias, a spray of phlox, etc. Consider
the magpie, the shiniest barrette.
And he said: the singing clown.
And she said: the fine print. Gotcha!
Barricades are essential, consciousness
is absolutely overrated. Match.com
is an excellent source of protein. When
I caught a song in her throat, the execution
was perfect. Everyone had a fine time.
Imagine the evolution of giraffes,
okapis, jackrabbits, arctic hares; melting
permafrost signifies latent dreamscapes?
Steam kills 99.9% of the lonelies

really? Which brings me to exhibit #13:
Dark Romanticism. Yes, the Argonauts,
or back when Sheldon met Clare,
in the atrium of the nursing home. Whatever
cradle rocks, yes? And the flautist, trilling
upon the memory of the divinity of grace.
actually believed the ordinance? *Popular
Mechanics* fixes everything. Oceanic
feelings can make them giddy.
Which orgasm? Are you kidding? Yes,
the necromancer charged the cellphone
towers, piercing the skin. As for the javelina,
the mustang, wild dogs, and Juarez, El Paso,
the defended border. Out upon all waterways,
a flickering ephemerality. Action wins pageants,
but not the swimsuit! For good reason: politics
is a sham, democracy is a sham, Democrats
are a sham, Republicans are a shame. Asylum
is asylum. To tickle the fancy bone, imagine
phallic symbols or porn. When independence
plucks the heartstrings, freedom rings in

the new normal? Sectors are reasonable.
Yes, the selection committee thanks you
for your consideration. Tattletales
may be hyperlinked and/or reposted.
the rising cost of Monsanto. Super seeds
are essential. Without an image diary,
killing off the children? And political
cabals, death squads, and mayhem. Murder
is everywhere. Consider the airborne
mercenaries of privatization. Yes,
since the onset of symptoms, my joy
traded in its humor. When bones
can no longer hold you up. Then:
the corpse, the backyard burial. A stray
bullet? Hotels are symbols of the republic.
and Paul Revere for sure. The mythmakers
fixed the generator in the boiler room. Nice!
Culture is absolutely essential, phenomena
are beloved by all. Yes, I sent the silly email.
And he said: no further communication

and she said: _____.
Afterward, we joined the United States
for plastic surgery? Believe the rattlesnake
or horse hobble cactus. When in Florida,
enjoy beaches and hotels and surf shops
or tee shirts. Knowledge personalizes
everything. For example, documentarians
need not apply pressure. Considerate
citizens dream the police dream
with uniform precision. A good job
for now? Younger than the times, but
opinionators are standing bipeds.
India may provide labor, and meaning
is absolutely essential. Surrealism
is often misinterpreted. Deconstruction
is often misinterpreted. The self is always
false, but imprisoned? Quest metaphors
can be stylish, with highlights. John Wayne
caught the electrician by the collar
and swung! The drunken bohemians

punctured the tissue of the social. Critics
raved, entered the mainstream. Babies
are incredibly pure and initially uncolonized—
until the dancer vomits? Yes, I have skipped
some developmental steps. Honestly,
since the onset of symptoms. Behold:
the yoga of online gaming. The hitman
preferred rhetoric in a *broader* capacity.
A killer among us, said the rapist,
and what about freedom? Ageism is bad,
the press secretary wailed. Willpower
is very useful. When spamming,
believe in economic forecasts,
and deficit spending. Your star or mine?
I mean, we only made it to the stairwell!
Whoa! In this streaming movie of our lives
cemeteries are beautiful; hoot owls hoot;
the moon is full. Forget the sycophants
and bootlickers, the brownnosers and
ass kissers. As for #13: the lackeys

and the hand wringers. Conmen

of action. Disable the inputs

destroy their habitat? Swamps filter

musketeers and intimidation. New Orleans

means different strategies. Artillery

or submachine guns? Target practice

with images of The Other. When

barbed wire ruled the earth, Destiny called

the ranch hand. The Marlboro Man

or his illegitimate sons? Daughters

of which Revolution? Is this English?

When I lost control of the feelings,

they logged out. A .45 GAP or

or .357 Magnum or .22 Remington or

.50 BMG? Cameras are absolutely essential.

Filmy romances, backlit explosions,

or flamethrowers, grenades, bazookas,

Uzis, WMD's: ecstatic catharses. Yes,

speak kindly to your subalterns. When

you choke on the truth, call 911

I should have been a Life Coach.

He said: you'll never get away with this!

And she said: I already have.

Oh snap! And children will believe

in the Red Hot Chili Peppers or racism,

the Mahatma or genocide. When suffering,

be quiet; remain absolutely still

and listen for the dream-birds nesting.

When in need, deliver the goods.

Politics will not integrate the system.

Managers will operate the system. The system

is very logical. Believe in functionality

and an assault rifle or human nature

or beauty. Etc. As for The Evidence: #14:

childlike wonder is absolutely essential;

hackers may enter crisis mode. Perception

solves everything, correct perception

is still the light and the way. I'm sorry,

a tie *is* a nice accessory. Believe in movie stars

and award ceremonies. Now that everything

is suffering. When carrying The Miracle,
offer an escape route, or place your head
directly into the clouds. When theophany
just isn't enough, push the button. Similarly,
paybacks, longstanding feuds. The embedded
journalist delivered barbarism to the masses,
with some compelling cinematography.
And he said: my burden is great.
And she said: the river is wide.
Consider the night heron, the pelican, or
giving thanks, alms. Before the tryst
behaving courageously? Litigation restores
the halcyon days. Since the onset of symptoms:
my sadness? Consider further refinements
to the suburbs, or the country. Yes, provide
care for the sickly, the meek, the misbegotten,
but remember: personal jets, yachts, helicopters,
tax-sheltered annuities, hedge funds, insider
trading, and monogrammed towels = the VIP
treatment. When someone finally shot
the prisoner, the movie rolled on

because of the absence of capital?
CGI and radar, waveguides or heat-seeking
missiles, UAVs. Finance majors need not
apply autocorrection. Beauty is simple
and despises aging! Engineering
is the new truth? Living is not easy
but goes on way too long. When government
services the oligarchs, technocrats may
suck it, or squeeze it, or eat it whole.
Collies or St Bernards? Man's best
foot forward. Always be closing

down. Consider *Fiddler on the Roof*
or *Casablanca* or even popular
culture? While everyone was suffering
in new ways. Consider craftsmen style?
Antiquing? Shooting stars deliver the Army,
Navy, Air Force, and Marines. Elections
are expensive. Senators prepare bodies
for death. Women and children are
pre-owned? The transformation of whiteness

and now that everyone is undocumented,

and untrustworthy, a bubbling cauldron

of sorcery! Consider how intuition mutates

like Ovid, pining, out on the Black Sea. See also:

the Strait of Hormuz, the Persian Gulf,

mesmerization, hypnotism, or telepathy in general,

drone strikes, rocket launchers, WMD's,

IEDs, and altars of remembrance. Order

is absolutely essential. Casting a shroud

of opportunism and effective self-promotion:

#15: The Final Episode. The return:

cold hard cash and a player to be named later.

An aperitif? Now that's what I call networking!

The messenger gasped, wrote his name

in blood. Prisons are uncorrectable. No,

because culture is wrong. Art mimes

that slightly sick feeling? The show must go—

See also: absolutism. You know, they say

the tip of the iceberg is only one eighth…

Dear Everyone: self-diagnoses

and Christopher Columbus, the natives.
Believe in leadership, categories,
emergency measures. Abraham Lincoln
is essential and also the Civil War,
emancipation, or civil rights in general.
See also: Jim Crow. New apartheids—
I emancipate the homeless.
I emancipate the uninsured.
I emancipate the multimillionaire
from this tyranny of social responsibility.
O, for Jesus to come back into all

American hearts and minds! The rise of
glitching, buzzing, beeping, clicking, vibrating
like a tremor? A tumor? Were I to reflect,
were I to feel? Since the onset of symptoms,
suffering, but not feeling; seeing
or more suffering? The end of suffering
is texting; status upgrades. Or more suffering.
Social engineering is absolutely essential.
No, because they don't own my heart

or something more scientific. Yes,

studies show that I am absolutely

mad? I put myself on a rocket ship

and said, "Au revoir!" Specialists

may deliver the antidote. Consider

neon, inflorescence, strobe lights,

and barhopping or clubbing. Disco lives.

And he said: Come here often?

And she said: This is a funeral! What?!

Corporations are expanding bionics.

some clarification, please. Yes, chat rooms

provide unfiltered hatred. Sanction the id?

for the politically unconscious? Now

that everything has been updated! No,

we sent the email. So *you're* the asshole?

Citizens Untied need not apply

free speech, or human rights. Treatment plans

provide amnesty? See also: drive-bys,

suicide bombers, hostage crises, and

well-armed property owners. Yes,

amazingly, snobbery persists! Mimicry
can be useful, as ornithologists have found
perplexing amounts of radiation in
impenetrable dreams. Force fields
KEEP OUT! Illegal aliens may squat
in our mythologies! Uprisings
will be edited out. When the entertainment
is boring, industry suffers. Consider
a 1972 Ford Mustang exploding
or a simulated strangulation, stabbing,
bludgeoning, impaling, or throat slitting.
Reality is absolutely essential
when producing effects. Scripts align.
decorative interiors, wish fulfillments
and #16: domestications, training manuals,
cleanliness, godliness, work ethics, politesse,
the observance of tradition. Consider
cardiovascular health and proper hydration.
Optimization? The Golden Age is not equal,
Love is not equal. Viral advertisements

surrender is youthless. Bathwater

is potable, as well as urine. Public excess

is an important strengthening exercise,

and may yield self-knowledge. Dragons

are essential elements of fantasy,

as well as princesses, princes, bloodlines,

and magic. The romance of the medieval

may require tax collecting and infamy

or chain mail, breastplates and dungeons

or grisly death. The olfactory system

is absolutely essential, and haute couture

is spill-proof: a fairy tale. Imagine

alternative vernaculars or statements

of intention. Storybook castles, moats

or drawbridges. The tarmac, runways,

engines propellers, de-icing fluid: systems

check. Contestants need not apply the anodyne.

Ergonomics, couch surfing, yoga mats

and upward mobility. Nothing signifies

when dressed for success. Imagine

the importance of the moon landing.
for generations to come! And tradition,
overstimulation, and finally: arousal,
sweet release. Genetically modified foods
should be burned. Consider the double-agent,
or Benedict Arnold vs. Edward Snowden
in an MMA death match! John Doe
and Jane Doe only skim the surface. Yes,
purposeful data migrations. Richard Nixon
is absolutely essential. Colonialism provides
organizers are standing bygones.
I emancipate war veterans.
I emancipate Bear Stearns.
I emancipate Wall Street.
I emancipate Countrywide and its CEO,
who should be shot on site? The baby? I
emancipate techies. Since the onset of symptoms,
halftime shows are essential expressions
of nationalism and propaganda. Bailouts? Yes,
America is too big to flail. Ride the tiger

or dream of the Messiah. Hark!

Deliverance waits for no man, Tiresias

said. Soon, Oedipus and Jocasta, well,

you know...! Quality or quantity? The masses

must be epitomized. Yes, streamlining

will do the trick. After the arbitration,

apply conditioner, moisturizing lotion

and antidepressants / deodorant.

Dear Everyone: deep in the heart

of the unconscious, there is a little

bomb that ticks. Tick, tick, tick.

bluebirds, redbirds or the mass grave

and murder, airstrikes, and carnage,

mutilation, reprisals. All explosions

are similarly comforting. See also:

high-speed chases. The end is nigh! Resent!

When dreaming of world peace, one may also

salvage sea turtles or primeval forests. Deliver

more uncertainty? Would *you* disconnect

the wires? Poetry can be so beautiful

no, I do not wish to see the spreadsheet.

Now that everything is already edited,

you are over-programmed. No,

there is no connection in the great out-of-doors.

Yes, believe in the transformative power

of music, and falling towers. Or moonlight

and a nice digestif. When dying,

deliver some laughter. #17 or so:

The Collective Unconscious. Although

the work is meaningful, timeless, and energetic,

true beauty may result in prolonged

addiction. Confidantes are standing biopics.

This poem is a public service announcement:

mindfulness and magnanimity or

disfranchisement and destitution. Severance pay

makes time. So the sociopath found

an outlet. Rationalizations can be comforting,

like armchairs or psychotic hallucinations,

and sirens and fire trucks. Little boys love

machinery, roughhousing, taxonomies

yes, I should have been a consultant!

not to a bona fide naturalist! Mixing labor

with the land produces varietals

of human, as well as "certain communities,"

the insistence of closed systems. No,

further applications? Directions for use: (a)

purposeful detonation, or something more

filmic: a condor soaring, the Chrysler building,

storms on the high seas, glacial calving.

Used-up mythology? Seeing clearly

is absolutely essential, seeing double

a teachable moment. Other ideas include

tofurkey, yams, cylinders of jellied cranberry—

Specialization is more marketable now,

believe the regulators. Internal auditing

may save lives. And he said: the portfolio.

And she said: the children, my god the—

Nostalgia is absolutely essential

for online purchasing and grief management.

Everyone should deliver compassion,

an expression of our innermost selves.
Or the poor, and new forms of abuse
interrupted by lots of commercials. Imagine
the loving parasite, some Machiavellian
planning commission. As for the Ford F-150:
militarizing Detroit or St. Louis. See also:
a blueprint of the replicating suburbs.
Suburbs are absolutely essential. Yes,
suburbs, but classism is bad, really bad,
and people are not always nice. Suburbs
produce the mini-mall, or public zoo and
personal hygiene, moisturizers, gardening.
The idea of Pangaea? Yes, central
inferences include savagery, skullduggery,
maiming, and (b) social climbing. To reach
hearts and minds? Excess fluid, gas
or waste products, decorated landfills.
Dreams sometimes provide good reasons
for action; poisons can come true.
Contradictory messages are killing babies

bonus question: censorship or

a day at the spa? Not to mention #18:

failure of leadership. Urgency

is manufactured. Over the counter

alienation is essential. Myths = spectacle,

and graphic designers need not apply.

Programmers need not apply.

Online editors need not apply. The maniac

in the cabin, slow cooking barbecued pork

and ideas. Need not apply. Consider the arts

of dog fighting or solitary confinement?

J.S. Mill was right. Locke was right.

Hume was right. Kant was right.

Nietzsche was right. Foucault was right.

Schopenhauer was not nice. The miniseries

ran aground. The Age of Navigation

was again upon us. Dear Everyone:

you are a conditioned response. Why not

consider the sponsors? Eugenics may

provide a romantic getaway weekend

or (c) some positions may be modified
for the uninitiated. Travelogues
have achieved nirvana. Delirium
should be taken once a day. Or the danger
of "certain communities" and misreading.
and Steve and Felix and Sheldon
or the girls down at the luncheon. *You*
considered applying? Do it yourself
or pay for service. True comfort
is expensive but absolutely essential.
How spammers went viral. John Brown's
body and the folk tradition? Believe
in the shrinking middle class? Yes, sports
speak for everyone. Dear Everyone:
dentists need not apply gauze.
Now that everything has been documented—
producing some new elements. Polymers
staying hydrated? Elections stage
fright, and mood lighting. Or exploitation.
They were doing it in the public fountain,

and on the bus, and in the metro, and
on the steps of City Hall! Smartphones
are absolutely essential. And immediacy,
the death of subjectivity. Silicon
is everywhere! And towers collapse
when you consider professional
displays of power, or plumage. Seasons
can still be beautiful, and empires
like some people better than others. Choice
belabors the point. Maintenance?
labor is so personal. Important questions
include foreignness and just desserts.
As for (d): prognostics, metaphors,
and game theory. Implications
include werewolves and vampires
or organic, free range, grass-fed cattle. Or,
consider the rain its purifying symbolism.
Prey. The Golden Age of Information
is hosting the ceremony? Attendance is
mandatory. Opinions are longstanding

salutations! Seeing really is believing!
Positive identification? The body
in the river, bobbing, bobbing, bobbing.
Everything is relatable. In the future,
Ginger or Mary Ann? Coming soon:
the coast of Normandy. Neo-Nazis may
corner the market. Species survive
with underwater cameras, biodegradable
flesh, and concrete. When performing,
envision a thousand emissions of gamma rays,
and empirical research, extinctions. Yes,
someone *should* study that. Why
brandish the sword? The duration
of new historic battles. Roaming
for a hero? Again? Consider the rainforest
or softness, bath tissue, essential oils,
Barbados, Jamaica, the Virgin Islands, and
economy travel. Write everything down!
I should have been a middle manager.
And bankers are not responsible,

and CEO's are not responsible,

on the Hollywood Walk of Fame? Whoa!

Ever tried cliff diving? Well, filtration

is not a sexy process, but effectiveness

may require testosterone supplements!

Regarding the intangibles: rebranding

is absolutely essential coding. Naming

displays, a primary function. And #19:

escape clauses, getaway cars. Determinism

was dampened by neuroscience. Freeways

are absolutely essential and runways

express contrition? Stay in the fairway

or chat room? A functional filtration system

ordered the pandemic? Oracles dried

their eyes. Now *that* was a hard winter,

as disasters go. CPA's are not responsible.

CFO's are not responsible. Consider penicillin,

even. Should we even have that conversation?

And he said: The darkness is upon me.

And she said: I have found God

at the airport? Love was up in the air? No,
I would not care to be on your mailing list,
compatriots. Remember the Alamo
and yearly checkups. Stockholders
are not responsible, and need not apply
pressure. One small incision? Physical therapy
or neural plasticity? As for (e): Exercise
is absolutely essential. Or telekinesis.
Consider the Volkswagen, or 4x4's
and risk/reward scenarios. Statistics
create bitter citizens. Actuaries need not
apply lip gloss. The Board of Trustees
is not responsible, and is not terribly nice.
Allegories sprout archetypes. Foreignness
may provide discomfort. Ethnic enclaves
may inject the labor force with hope. Questions
may arise with painful urination. Powerbrokers
may slurp it raw or suck it with hot sauce. Consider
the road crew, or poetry. Now that real life
has been spoken for, and is beyond repair

yes, diseases are inconvenient! Why
lament the lasting effects? Contritions
are not for everyone. Dear Everyone:
give weight loss pills a try? Time presses
on formations of cruelty. The Management
oversees end-of-the-year blowouts
and selfies. Debauchery and sexcapades
celebrate populism. Believe in tradition
at all costs. Reposting or retweeting
extends careerism. Networking may provide
greed, disdain, conformity, spite,
and meritocratic ideals. Capitalism loves
the image of itself. Dear Everyone:
when producing hits, new values are
old values, and easily justified, but
Sunday afternoons can just get away!
Politics is cleaner in the academy. Consider
bedsores or last rites and sadness,
emojis and shared suspicions/plotting.
I should have been a fact checker

from far away, the countryside is idyllic.

From far away, the road is a mirage.

From far away, memory is incomplete.

From far away, the past.

From far away, the city appears unified.

From far away, the narrative arises.

From far away, pain is ineffective.

From far away, politics happen.

From far away, categories appear.

From far away, essentialisms.

From far away, the idea of love.

From far away, the target audience.

From far away, the instinct, pre-wrapped.

From far away, the crux of history.

From far away, the practical application.

From far away, the foreseeable future.

From far away, new forms of war.

From far away, the operating system.

From far away, the emerging market.

From far away, no one is responsible

which brings me to #20 and #21:

the sun and the moon: Hatha yoga.

Anywhere you can go, a suicide bomber

or school shooter. The Detective returned

with an image of the Police-dream.

And John Doe said: passion.

And Jane Doe said: lack of passion.

Ordinarily, if the shoe fits, or the condom

and theme parks, vista points, brochures.

When bobbing to the surface, splutter,

wave, or hit 'Reply All.' Dear Everyone:

imperialism is really not fair, but may

provide free reeducation. Or post-production

selling points. Niche markets may open

superstores. Consider the yelping sea lions

and barrels of nuclear waste. Beauty is

similar to everything else. The Dark Ages

and Renaissance contributed to this report.

out of context? There are no sources

I should have been a programmer

therefore, unprecedented measures may
deploy the paradigm shift. Conspirators
are standing by their statements. Thus,
plot, character, tone, POV, and special effects
are essential. For example:
drone strikes, evacuations, refugee crises,
starvation, mass rape, contamination, disease,
ritual mutilation, slavery, child prostitution,
terror. Ergo, soundtracks may contain
stroking, rubbing, tentative nibbling,
deep, involved kissing, passionate moaning,
sweet rhythmic lovemaking. Dear Everyone:
would you care for a courtesy reminder
or magical thinking? Last but not least,
(f): destroy this poem and all other disclaimers.
Oh no! It wasn't the airplanes. It was Beauty
killed the Beast. And if you must know,
I am in love with you. To conclude: nothing herein
is admissible as evidence. We are adjourned.
You are free to move about the cabin

DESCRIPTIVE ANALYTICS

OR

THE HIGHWAY OF THE PAST

lather up. Some salacious inventories
are organizational mediations? Why
lament the talisman? Consider magic
or Cubism or Futurism or militarism.
All too true. Ordinarily, the flesh wound
focuses the attention. I've transplanted
matching pairs, emptied the attic. Dust
gatherers at the road show. Nymphs lift,
scattering dandelion seeds. Yes,
when the first one died. Sense blanks
on positions. Impositions. Get the picture
or history repeats itself. Everything
endeavors to the cadaver, or leaves
for posterity. The homesteaders believed
in wagons, barrels, corn husks, or ploughs?
No further investments? The valueless
demand conference calls. Privacy is
untranslatable. Along the highway of the past
truncations, deletions. Down on the ground
of love. When the calls came in

predictable epiphanies. Squandering

extensions of public space: war—

As for the rest? Recliners, sofas,

ornate pillows, even. Willows blowing

apart the government. Research helps

carry everything. Baskets and disposable

geographies of the self. Some saccharine

note-passing, breathless, tingly sensations,

or improper sharing. Delight in sex

or fuel aesthetic bliss: deliberate.

Time-sensitive materials will not be returned.

When creating your past lives, responses

may undergo transformation. Cities

of destruction; systematic debilitation

the soundtrack of the past? Love

sleeps in childhood. You arise

with considerable provocation. As for

jpegs, gifs, gigabytes, electronic equipment:

the selfie, voiceover, some petting,

licking, or necking. No further questions

and damage. When alarms scattered
the bodies in the street. Smoke assures
correct behavior, and politics delivers
screaming: "My baby!" "My baby!"
In the postcard: settlers, homesteaders,
adventurers, buckaroos, explorers, privateers,
conquerors. The natives. Roadside bombs
are serious business! Rednecks
need not apply. Imagined histories
in post-production mode. When internalized,
the inoculation may take decades. No,
we are beyond pleasantries. No,
poetry is not a vehicle. The pressurized clot
of the systolic. I am a protostar, equilibrated
and refined, well-mannered. Resolutions
believe intentions. The present
is always coughing slogans? Furthermore,
unusable footage. When the calls came in
cartographies of the self. In your letter
be sure to provide comfort, a sense of hope

or pills, prescriptions. The messenger
waylaid the barbarians. Time burnt a hole
in their whereabouts. Why admonish
dream houses? The princess arose and wept
mathematical "resemblance." So,
terror lies in wait. The operation is clean
in its way, or manual pumping. Jam
these halos of the few. Why torch
the Amazon? Swim the Orinoco,
depending on the discard. Trash collects
regional pastimes; following tradition
may aggravate injuries. Teleology
seals everything, like Revelations or
return flights. Disable impermanence,
or desertification. AWOL? When considering
the Gestapo? Or the KGB? The police-dream
is beyond efficient! Think about it:
martial arts or banditry? Descendants
carry on the conditions. When lost,
brandish the symbolic realm. Yes,

where love rotted! Disease tracking

procedures: spay or neuter your territorial

markings. When the calls came in

with Barbara and the other Clare,

the last vacation! The halcyon days

ravaged the organs. Someone sang

through the pain. This factory

of particular resonance. Products

question the invasion, or the eradication

or the rebuilding process. Ultra-reality

mansions, people of import. Magazines

are photogenic, and can be

easily reprogrammed. Consider

asking the difficult questions. No,

I would not like to see your recent edit

and furthermore, calories. No business

as usual, the lackeys. Yes men!

Yes, the arrangement was delivered.

an impromptu speech? Why I believe

in potlucks, picnics, clam bakes, fish fries—

and barbarism. Things to fear include:

capsizing, holocaust, radioactivity

excessive telephoning, extension cords

murder, bloodshed, mayhem, drowning

in the bathtub, airplanes, the Collective

Unconscious, leaders, followers,

and lawmakers. Debutantes miss out—

When remembering the good old days,

take the trick! Argumentation syncs

cover-ups. Michelangelo painted the frame

of this poem, and poetry is a chapel

or brothel. Who can say? Poetry is

the holy sex worker of language? Well...

instigators are standing by. Bystanders die

in tense exchanges, remanded reports, too,

paper shuffling. The excessive function

of gender and sexuality. In *The Republic*,

cherubic, heroic, boys, or also *The Satyricon*?

Giton complained to the local authorities.

Consider monopolies, cartels, business as

unusual. Yes, they have now become white,

stuck in a photo album somewhere,
or the facility. Flooding may occur
or memories return, and shock therapy
or intellectualizing death? No,
the blessed Virgin. Ordinarily,
hubristic hyperbole and backscratching
or the hell of gridlock. New myths
love delicate children, and babies. Reasons
can be found, like lasers or microchips.
What witch hunt? Believe
what you want. Since the onset
of symptoms and self-flagellation
or public embarrassments, apologies.
Moral fiber? With respect to
practical jokes, or disaster relief,
skin doesn't last. Silken sheets
for a deathbed? Spruce it up a bit.
The vagus nerve soothes cargo, trucks
in troubles. You pass yourself around.
Your life is sound-byte culture

when in doubt, provide healthcare

coverage or costumes. Clothing makes

the Pomeranian? Traffic cops may

offer calisthenics. The good life

is always cracked up to be

porcelain gods, or lost marbles, even. Yes,

imagine a clay jar, painted in fantastic

rituals. Philistinism places catcalls

and operates video games. Pundits

shape everything. Imagine Gandhi

coloring between the lines! Death by

sarcasm, or talk show host. Furthermore,

the sanctity of marriage and military

occupations. Side-effects may eclipse

the margin of error, human nature, developing

phantasms. When the calls came in

to perform the eulogy. Which music

will play? "O love!" The portentous rooms

are signs. Semiotics cannot soothe

the ongoing extinction. Or the lack

of tangible detail. Imagine the pear tree

or many varieties of scrubs. Believe

in airports, and the Econo Lodge

or The Radisson or the Super 8, Motel 6

or the Holiday Inn. Drifting, variation

or the hybrid? Poetry is bloodless

and not guilty. But downsizing

may prevent clotting. Conquering

these territories of the heart. No,

I do not wish to receive your newsletter,

an inventory of the self? For example,

stretchers, gurneys, HMO's and

coffins, pedestals, tripods, camera cases,

microphones, pocket handkerchiefs,

and blasphemy? The pedophile lies

in wait. An oceanic restructuring of pleasure,

and its coordinates. When navigating

The Body, be sure to lubricate emphatically.

Voyeurism is the new couch surfing

the new landed gentry. Once upon a time

so isolationist? Now that everything

is the onset of symptoms. Literature is

organized religion. Burial mounds

may be unearthed. *Boo! Surprise!* Consider

the dung beetle, the piss ant, cave bats, spiders,

sulfuric leakage, and Pluto. Persephone

complained to the local authorities. No,

I do not wish to receive a complementary T-shirt

or travel bag. Carryon items indicate

separation anxiety. In her diary entries,

the silences of history. Beauty =

gentrification? Things to fear include:

maniacs, terrorists, accidents, saturated fats,

sugar, Iran, Iraq, smokers, carbon monoxide,

kidnappers, rapists, the everyday, young, white

boys, the homeless, street gangs, police officers,

boll weevils, locusts, termites, Winter Weather

Advisories, meteorites, interplanetary debris.

No, you have not received authorization

to the heart of the matter? Love
is passing, and passing through.
Now that everything has been documented
or freeze-dried. Elements include:
festivals, cartoons, newspaper clippings,
old songs, figurines, envelopes,
stamps, coins, memories, artificial
memories, and ideas of time. Certainly,
safe travels! Observe containment policies.
When persistence argues ineffectively, charm
may open doors. Opportunism is inviting
and sell them on a dream! Confiscate
unused urgencies, or redirect the impulses
and purchase power. The ordinance
threw a surprise party! Awesome!
In the video recording, evidence of unity
and wistful thinking. Whoa! Sometimes
I get these oceanic feelings for human labor,
client-centered protocol. In the dream, begin
by erasing? Display the proper gratitude

cease or desist! Insider raiding
fetish objects and social media inlets
or personalized license plates?
and tempo, duration, modulation,
or morning calisthenics. The yoga
of consumerism. When the life force
withers, and natural metaphors cycle out,
push-button convenience. Touch
is exceptional, like gifted children,
the military, or privacy. Consider the killdeer
or mourning dove. And Hector bloodied
on the plains of Ilium. Now that
encrypted men produce nationalism,
we must harvest these rhizomes of empire!
Yes, individuality sells! Consider
the firm, the film, the advertisement,
the public service announcement,
and mythmaking. Articulators are
stranding by. Believe in screensavers,
the silent majority, the general wellbeing

well, what *is* wealthy? Or tempers flare,

reenact the perfect crime? The dead

detective. In the burning river,

cameras are absolutely essential.

When love lands the gentry, and dreams

articulate impossible genders. Now

that everything has been documented

in the cropped picture? False dichotomies

are perfectly accessible reading. So,

1000 Places to See Before You Die or

the latest scholarship? Think tanks

provide limits. Inquiries funnel

passionate resistance, the commander

scans, militaristic screens. Skin

surrenders to culture, and culture—

Listen: believe in breeding, or the Self

passes away. We will proceed as planned

with data mining. Exceeding expectations

is the new killing machine. Yes,

I should have been an accountant

some real what-if thinking. Researchers
profile The People. Information
may be used against you. Abandon
the torrent. Now that everything
has been documented, different positions
may spruce up your love life. Imagine
a talking head in leather or bondage
preaching family values. Since the onset of
overproduction, inappropriate confessions,
some exciting disavowals, deletions
scrubbing and processing fees. Ordinarily,
people are not nice, but charming
and definitely salesworthy. For instance,
uninterrupted service and truly impressive
inventories! Always provide solace
and a soundtrack. Outside, the playground,
the dog park. Beyond? Seagulls, seagulls.
Ordinarily, everybody is feeling fine
but difficulty is essential. Dear Everyone:
mind control or impulse regulation

narratives are lies. Consider rebellion
or anomie, or more effective anarchy
domestic terrorism, even. Acts
of beauty are required, manic gestures
are required, discordant sentences
are required. No assembly is required.
And jogging or stretching, swimming
and protein shakes. Muscle memory
just takes over! Believe in disease, certain
doom, and flagellations of every kind.
As for the weather: lots of sun
and mirth. Devices and pheromones
and new applications. The Central
Post-Intelligence System? O, love!
and the hangover jitters. Participate
in mass consumption, or live long
and die trying. When resistant bacteria
collide with reality? Yikes! Discomfort
is not nice, and flagellations may
become the new you. And the new you

ordinarily, I am generous, somewhat shy,
and extremely handsome. Torture
solves everything. And self-effacement
or inflicting pain. But repose, couches
sofas, armchairs, and/or extra blankets
can solve problems, too. Finding solutions
or medication. And shapes, graphs,
figures, numbers, factors, proportions,
and ratios, portfolios, actuarial science,
informants, spies, sharpshooters, juntas,
drones, air strikes, bombings, and
ideological structures. The detail-oriented
need not apply. And public servants
may be misguided. Believe in enemies
or make time and money! Do not trust anyone
legendary or ageless. Seek illumination
in the blogosphere, site maps, and traffic.
Consider organized remission, venality,
or retaliation. Justify everything
before disarmament. Imagine death

no,

I would not like to receive a free one-week trial,

now that everything has been documented.

Remember all those evenings under the stars.

Remember all those evenings around the campfire.

Remember all those evenings with sing-a-longs and weed.

Remember all those drunken evenings, if possible.

Remember all those catastrophic evenings.

Remember all those therapeutic evenings.

Remember all those memorable evenings

covered in silence. Along the highway of the past,

the wind, the dust, burning buildings,

and savagery. Repercussions are standing by

doomsday scenarios. The hero went up

in a rocket of flame. Lobbyists, loyalists, and

special interest groups need not apply.

Things to fear include: ergonomics,

efficiency, compunction, technology,

God, women's bodies, men's bodies,

mental illness, cemeteries, the atmosphere

and large swaths of The Middle East.

FREE TIBET! Wisdom is impermanence,

etc. When the calls came in

new forms of imperialism. Organic initiatives

dismember the spirit animal. For instance,

the dead messenger, the dead detective.

Clues are everywhere. Fashionistas see—

Dear Everyone: consider origin myths

and cancer, cholera, chemotherapy,

or Neil Diamond. Organization

is repetition, when something stirs

the passions, the humors, the heebie-jeebies.

But nothing here is funny, splenetic,

melancholic, or personable. You dislike

federations and demagogues, yes,

but magic? Telepathy solves quotients

rebuses, crosswords, Sudokus,

and North Carolina, Tennessee, South Carolina,

colonialists, armed resistance, guerrilla

methodologies. The professional

or professionalism? Efficiency
is absolutely essential, and pleasing
conformism? Intractable behaviors and
poetry are easily outmoded. When war
offers its hand, and shared commitments:
behold, The Rupture. Dear Everyone:
call me sometime? Ordinarily,
I am not especially chatty, but wise
to paranoia. Pilots, episodes, reruns,
and conspiracy theories. No,
I am not interested in taking a brochure
or providing information. Just because.
When you stop to consider cacti, lizards,
and desertification, planetary debris.
just outside the frame? History
and the beautiful past. Nostalgia
prevents natural disasters and suicide
or causes inflammation, itchiness,
and blockages. The barricades
are illusions: fully realized images

goodbye, Sheldon. Goodbye, Steve.

Goodbye Clare. Goodbye, the other Clare.

Goodbye, Barbara. Goodbye, Emilio.

Goodbye, Felix. Goodbye, Randy.

Index A: flamethrowers, fire-retardant suits,

astronauts, musical instruments, grenades,

SCUBA divers, the great white shark,

the archetypal islander. When considering

transmigration or owls, Hermes

and so forth. When paparazzi succeed.

As for the money shot: _____!

Begin with light calisthenics, jog in place

and punch out imaginary villains. Yes,

always be closing. Always come prepared!

Believe in yourself! Believe in your dreams!

strewn along the highway of the past.

Since the onset of symptoms, I have seen—

so we sent the email: send. Bcc: No,

I am not interested in reading your literature.

Yes, I should have been a sports reporter

so we traced the email. Tour guides are

stranding biometrics. I got in touch

with myself, and the ever-breakable past.

When we lived in the future,

the less said the better! Stretching the truth

warms hearts and minds. Rumors

always take shape. Depending on survival,

defense budgets condition proprietary citizens.

Alarms are exceptional. People are

not very nice in summer, or winter or

Tucson, Phoenix, Flagstaff, Tempe,

and the chain restaurants! My God! Conditions

apply to college. Or else you might believe

those perpetrators. But transparency and

festivals or masquerades and the importance

of exercise, diet, and proper hydration;

regular evacuations are also useful. Lamentations

or sincere stupidity? Horses, silos, and fields

are beautiful, on the highway of the past.

Something scribbled in the margins

ordinarily, one must banish both fertility
and sameness. Index B: recharging,
notes to self, panic (small and medium sized),
placement, updating, outdating,
loyalty, betrayal, things in the attic, things
in the basement, water heaters, radiators,
ephemera. Beyond the highway of the past
synthetic tissues, androidal premonitions.
some nicer weather! But hopefully,
the prognosis rattled around inside
another important documentary. A pill
for what ails you. Consider the smell of coffee,
the smell of the homeless, of tent cities,
the sound of jingling. When the lonelies strike,
consider earnestness, the multiple exposures
of your uniqueness. Logicians
need not apply. Also that hospital smell
and flesh-eating bacteria. Maggots
can be beautiful, in their own special
revolution. Would you believe that

now that history is full of ulterior motives

and trivia, or something to say

at cocktail parties. And furthermore,

out on the highway of the past,

pleasing road signs, unseen systems

and freedom and romance and opportunity

and bitter disappointment. If you believe

the owners, interconnectivity can be personable.

And the unspeakable, agreed-upon silences,

pursuits of happiness. Nostalgia cures

back pain, frozen shoulders, twitching, anemia,

and vertigo. Or thought bubbles, screaming:

"My baby!" "My baby!" "Please help!"

A federal holiday? Index C: ideology,

historical apologies, restitution,

peace accords, agreements, treaties, pacts,

and falsified documents. Otherwise, feed

the anarchist in the living room, or raise

some hellions for children. Someone screaming

bloody murder, mayhem and carnage

and gore. Explosions make everything
a little brighter. Dear Everyone:
it has been so long since we last
saw each other and in the intervening
years we have grown apart and yet
I feel closer to you now than ever.
Perhaps that has to do with genetics
or Leo Tolstoy's *The Kreutzer Sonata*,
or how we are both now on Facebook.
Can you believe how much the world
has changed since we were kids???
Although we are so far apart
I feel like not even a day has passed!
how like us, like us! Ah life! Are you
ready for Jesus? The End draws Nigh.
And can you believe Shirley&Fred,
Bill&Rita, Susan&Phil, Anne&Mick,
Connie&Connie, and Eleanor!!!
Please post more photos of your vacations
and pets and important rites of passage,

including death and aberrant behaviors.

Sincerely,

I am not interested in special offers or coupons.

Since the onset of symptoms,

I have become maniacal, certifiably

cavalier, in the face of dearth. Otherwise,

death is everywhere, and acts of contrition

may not apply. Catalogues are useful.

or futility gods? We crafted the agenda

in the midst of life. Afterward, coming home

to fruition. Monopolizing disfranchisement

seasonal bribery; Exxon or Chevron? Ordinarily,

I am eager to please and somewhat witty

or not. Believe in the power and the glory

of advertising and park benches, trains,

and the continuity of weather. Even so,

Index D: home insurance agents, realtors,

auto insurance agents, consultants,

life coaches, fitness gurus, the NRA,

and Haley, Idaho. Grown ups are not nice

I should have been a chief executive
floating on a psychedelic breeze
with hummingbirds. The small intestine
and large intestine or a four-chambered
heart and/or stomach, depending
on magic and spiritualism. Leverage
works every time, and sensationalism,
where everybody wants to be someone
or somewhere else. Consider the American
crow and treetops, nature hikes, icy cold
and frozen lakes. The last isolation
on a fault line? First message: Do you
or someone you know *message deleted*. And
grisly death, torture, mayhem, bloodshed, book
burning, cunning, terror, sensory deprivation.
Index E: demonology, phrenology,
cosmology, angelology and religiosity,
spirituality, prognostication and the pleasures
of accuracy and proper satellite positioning.
I should have been a missing person

ordained in wrongness, false alibis,

and television hair. Ordinarily, surrender

may occur, now that everything has been

modified and / or persecuted. The correct

position is always my favorite. Feelings

are helpful. On the picture wheel,

falcons, hawks, eagles, raptors

of every variety. When you see broken beauty,

or broken will or broken humanity,

residing in temporary housing, broken beds

broken hysteria, broken dreams

and diminishment. Because malnutrition

and waterways, breaking: the open sea.

See also: mermaids, parasites, microbes

of any persuasion. Lancelot, this enveloping mist

or whinnying, clucking, a sparrow song,

and greeting cards. When lost, I

dispute resolutions. Memory Lane may be

found in bedrooms, living rooms, hallways;

the brilliant constructions of the dream

next message: Are you *message deleted*
or public executions, posses, lynchings, militias,
police violence, the presumed guilty, the presumed
incompetent, the presumed degenerate. Roadkill
may be viewed exclusively metaphorically—
and also poetry. Demons and angels
are certainly Romantic, but sometimes deadly
guerrillas. When articulation fails, scream
through speech itself. Have faith, or faithlessness.
what you bring with you? God is in
personality tests, indexes of happiness
and filth, gore: everlasting desecration. Horizons
indicate damage-control, or radiation spikes;
inspections may be necessary. Pursuant to
Atlantis and other morphologies, bonus tracks
and liner notes. Index F: the incubus, the succubus,
the roc, the cockatrice, the Grim Reaper. When
you stop to consider The Valkyries' flight,
shock jocks, celebrity weddings, luxury resorts,
or discovery? Fiction is its own dream

and misuses of the human project?

Imagine that you are a sharpened pencil,

that you are writing your own story

or something more advanced: pathology.

You may wish to explain all as unity:

microcosm, macrocosm, gradient, differential.

Instructions will not be available. When burning

children run across the advent. Ordinarily,

techies motivate latent brain-ware. If yes,

imagine 11% or 12%, or the yoga of tradition

and emotions. The symphony plays on,

the opera holds forth, the ballet is leaping

into the Petri dish or the compost heap?

Next message: Are you ready? The End

draws Nigh *message deleted*. Evangelists

need not apply exegesis or silver iodide—

the kidneys may fail, or the liver. Politicians

may consider laser light shows. Messengers

deliver the diatribe? The llama or the alpaca

or some other organizational principle

no, I would not like to get involved,

although memorization is a lost art, considering

projection models, malicious code, syntax

errors, firewalls, encryption. Images are

absolutely essential. The heart may fail, or

governmental regulations. Objects explain

when rising to the absolute abstraction.

Consider the Heermann's gull, oil spills,

disasters are best forgotten. Yes, a triumph

of the human spirit. Next message:

Hi there! I'm returning your *message deleted*,

and logos, statistics, last year's fashion

and models. Index G: lists, indexes,

precepts, bodies, forms of death

and torture, reasons to kill, plagiarism,

sampling, hotels, restaurants, airports,

and symptoms. O love is a many-slandered—

Well, some exaggerations are useful. Panic

explains everything too quickly. Yes,

confront the death of the ideal, the dream

of conscience. The eyes may fail, the ears

may fail, or repositories of meaning

may become unbearable. As spring nears,

the polar bear sleeps on its floe of extinction,

and the lymph nodes may fail and cancer

grows beauteous evenings? Imagos

explain everything succinctly. When you consider

The Good Samaritan or the self-made man

or tenderness. Out on the highway of the past,

suicide bombers, lone gunmen, arsonists,

and the maximum security stimulation

of pleasure centers. One allegory

leads to the promised land. Yearning

and poetry are figments of the imagination. Yes,

the arteries may fail, the lungs may fail,

the pancreas may fail, the memory may fail,

or, consider the ten best films of the year.

Who made *that* decision? Retribution

sells. Observation towers need not apply

flickering lighthouses, or oceanic feelings

the keepers of the wish list, the cure. Keep
the faithful off the grass. Tempters may
flare, and flamethrowers, hydrogen bombs
and chemical warfare, cyber-attacks
and hip hop, house music, R&B, country—
(My saddle? My hat? My boots?)
the pacemaker may fail, the stent may fail,
chemotherapy may fail rehab may fail,
or experimental treatments. Poetry
is absolutely essential, in this case,
but banished! Or pre-qualified, statements
can always be prepared. Consistency
can be convincing. Sea foam, sea spray,
the sea breeze, seascapes and the benefits
of a healthy diet. See? She holds the child
to her breast, but memories shift, fill, replace,
and void, and the present is a mouthful
of atoms, sub-atomic particles, and pixie dust.
When myths regulate behavior, or the police-dream,
spectacles are essential. I should have been

a powerbroker or pawn broker.

Next message: *message deleted*. Index G:

bar graphs, pie charts, projection models,

simulated results, The Mainframe, the Rorschach,

and situation comedies. Standards explain

everything. Dear Everyone: over-explainers

and over-sharers need not apply. Yes,

as for the healing powers of excavations

of the Imaginary: the Ingénue bounded

into the Enchanted Forest, with

the manifest Pleroma. When you consider

body hair, or flaking skin, mucous membranes,

pus, MRSA, staff infections, abscesses,

and ecosystems. The nervous system

may fail, or the bladder may fail or

beauty. Out on the highway of the past—

Goodbye, James Taylor. Goodbye,

Paul Simon. Goodbye, Carly Simon.

Goodbye, Neil Young. Goodbye,

Kenny Rogers. Goodbye, Carole King

hello, Paul McCartney. Windows
program everything. Immensity registers
for emergencies. Because the present
is impossible and operating systems
are implausible. A throbbing, or discomfort?
The surgery may fail, the medication may fail,
the pacemaker may fail, prayer may fail, leaders—
pageants answer the wrong questions. Slogans
may eradicate useful bacteria. Index H:
festivals, carnivals, street fairs, house parties,
sports contests, The Circus, rock concerts,
riots, protests, and the status quo. Dear Everyone:
it was truly great catching up last weekend,
it had been way too long but could you believe it
we were exactly the same except for Barbara
and I hadn't realized at the time that those days
were as important as they are to me now
and it gives you a little faith in the world
to know that good people are out there or
effectively placed products. Movies to watch:

goodbye, Paul McCartney. Peace and love

and dancing? Karaoke mimics. Living

is easy, and sad, but people are not nice

or fulfilling. Misery can be useful

and startling, like nudity in the mini mall

or gunshots outside an upscale restaurant

or terminal disease or domestic abuse. Consider

going on safari! Death hangs upon the wall

and carnage, mayhem, dismemberment,

and assassinations or beheadings. Ritual

hatred explains everything. When reducing

ethnic cleansing, on the highway of the past

nostalgia is the crown jewel of pornography.

Consider the executioner properly warming up

with jumping jacks, calisthenics, lunges,

dual masturbation, and threesomes. Furthermore,

like images, updates and commentary. Hello,

Paul McCartney. The large intestine

or the small intestine may fail, all meaning may—

Ergo, thrusting motions, or stroking, caressing

no way! Next message: Get over here
now *message deleted*. Bone density
may fail, red blood cells may fail, white
bloods cells may fail, and nationalisms.
Index H: nature poetry, nature photography,
nature hikes, nature painting, and non-native
weather, non-native species, the hydra,
the amoeba, the oocyte. Firepower
can be very convincing, and musculature
emboldens the skeleton. Imagine industries
and the industrious, professional killers
and mayhem, bloodshed, mass murder
and new questions of ethics. Plantations
indicate optical illusions. The Border
is a vista point? Reparations? Apologies?
very well. In the photograph, she smiles.
Out on the highway of the past, ghosts
attend the picture show. In many poses
rhythmic breathing may increase stimulation.
Yes, proper flagellation takes time,

effort, and money. Beauty is ageless,

although strings may be attached. Mood

lighting explains everything. Authorship

or the intentional fallacy? Trolling

for all intents and purposes. No,

I do not wish to become a gold star member.

Goodbye, Paul McCartney. Tracksuits

or tennis shoes? Well, chemo may fail,

the tracheotomy may fail, the angioplasty

may fail, or the defense administration

may provide provocative imagery. Yes,

The Unconscious is a launch pad, but

conformism comes in many shapes and sizes,

like wisdom. Behavior is the problem.

Production values may vary. Poets and artists

need not apply. Theoretical applications

explain everything incompletely. Or, deliver

something objectionable? Believe Greek myth,

Roman rhetoric, some version of Abrahamic

religion and American exceptionalism

if at all possible. Or, uncomfortable silence
explains everything. Consider the 1980's:
Goodbye, Katarina. Goodbye, Debi. Goodbye,
Midori. Goodbye, Dorothy. Goodbye, Peggy.
Goodbye, Sonja. Photoshop shapes
essentialism. Dear Everyone: the yoga
of disaster and energy-fields: consider *Star Wars*
and all post-apocalyptic ideation. Supremacy
is convincing, but is not very thoughtful
and can be so challenging! The absent father
and overbearing mother may produce
video rentals, fast food, low-stakes poker or
time-wasting. Accessories indicate leverage
and microscopes, telescopes, regulatory committees
at the furthest reaches of the empire! Who
did you imagine burning at the stake? Often,
remedies inhere in the structure of disease,
like Crusaders? Believe in pharmaceuticals
but not historical apologies, restitution,
symbolic offerings, valor, ardor, charm,
lineage, destiny, or violence as an answer

to violence. Surveillance is the new

spectacle? Big brother and little brother

insure truthfulness, or else. Got it? When

someone is always wrong. Atonement may

reach out to your inner child? I am sorry,

inner child from 1978-1982. I am sorry,

inner child from 1983; 1984-1995. I am sorry,

inner child from 1996. And 1996-present.

I am sorry, inner child of the always-past. I am sorry,

inner child of the ever-present: whom I cannot look

in the eye, whom I cannot embrace, whom I cannot love.

I am sorry, body from 1975-1982. I am sorry, body

from 1983, 1984-1986, 1987-1990, 1991-1995;

I am very sorry, body from 1996. And 1996-present

I am sorry, all bodies of the future. Meditation

explains without explaining? Research translates

the cosmos inaccurately. Ordinarily, I am

easygoing, open-minded, gregarious, fun-loving—

I should have been a prophet, or park ranger

pursuant to the policy claims of Mr. Yes,

vis-à-vis the dead detective, the slain messenger:

Index I: refineries, platforms, extractions,

production, post-production, tankers,

tankards, tanks, pipelines, hoses,

aircraft carriers, the Persian Gulf,

eyewitness reports, falsification,

beta tests, gamma rays, Greek philosophy,

and duration, humanity, thought itself

and flesh wounds, shrapnel, night terrors,

gunshot wounds, burning pitch,

rocket launchers, bazookas, poison,

prison, surveillance, and preemptive strikes.

Extraneous feelings? Talk therapy is

absolutely essential. Since the onset of symptoms,

people are not nice. Consider this questionnaire:

1. Have you ever been convicted of a felony?

2. What is your mother's maiden name?

3. Are you a permanent resident of the United States?

4. Do you use drugs or alcohol on a daily basis?

4A. If yes, please explain: _____

_____

_____

_____ .

5. Have you ever been out on the highway of the past?

Now that everything has been documented,

radical subjectivities, ironies, and terror. No,

I would not like to receive biweekly reminders.

and ephedrine. In the album, fear of mediocrity,

The Self. Disease clarifies everything.

Whoosh. Intimacy, willpower, a lack of desire,

understanding and forgiveness. Morality

is absolutely essential. Consider villains,

monsters, ogres, trolls, troglodytes, kobolds,

and Five Star resorts! The Good Life

is soothing, when conditioned. Ordinarily,

I am loving, thoughtful, somewhat naïve

but vengeance, antinomy, extremism,

outdoor weddings, champagne, and arboreta.

I saw babies in the wreckage, burned

so we sent the email. Next message:

Do you or someone you know *message deleted.*

Index J: the BMW, the Volkswagen,

the Ford, the Chrysler, the Chevrolet,

the Audi, the Nissan, the Honda,

but not the Toyota or the Mitsubishi and

excisions, autocorrections, and tracking

devices are absolutely essential.

Dear Everyone: have you seen the pictures

I posted on FB from last weekend at the beach

(so cray!) and our big night out on the town

with Federico, the horny exchange student

and Lazaro, his ultra-American friend,

and the dumb bros with the hydroponic

and the biker gang, the goths and their pit bulls?

Next message: Hello? Hello? *Message deleted.*

Collateral damage? Children are targets

and unprepared for war and easily abused

by the self-righteous and the god-complexed.

I should have been a paper pusher

report finds many new positions

may satisfy! Furthermore, tax lawyers,

shell companies and banality, conformism,

or establishments. Believe in camaraderie

or exclusionism? Capitalists are wrong.

Communists are wrong. Conservatives are

traditionally wrong. Liberals are openly wrong.

Independents are freely wrong. Authoritarians

are absolutely wrong. Oligarchies are

expensively wrong. Theocracies are

infinitely wrong. Progressives are futuristically

wrong. Technocracies are programmed

all wrong. Anarchists are paradoxes and

also not paradoxes? Libertines are selfishly

wrong. Constitutionalists are literally wrong.

The unaffiliated are delusional and wrong,

but possibly very nice. Kleptocrats always

steal the show! Pacifists.... Out on the highway

of the past, chance encounters, kismet,

happenstance. No, poetry is not political,

despite the facts. Hemoglobin or clotting

may fail, seatbelts may fail, the body

may fail, or the mind may fail, and literature,

the past, present, and the future may all fail.

Me personally? Camera angles explain

everything, and editing and duration. No,

the insurance will not cover this one! Fiction

distributes the commonwealth, and Marx

was right and not right. Freud was

right and not right. Jung was not really right

but interesting. George Washington

was always considerate. Thomas Jefferson

was not always considerate, with exceptions.

Millard Fillmore and James K. Polk are

forgettable. Index K: East Germany (defunct),

West Germany (defunct), Prussia (defunct),

The Confederacy (partly defunct), Upper Volta

(defunct), Burma (defunct), Czechoslovakia

(defunct), Yugoslavia (defunct), Manchuria (defunct),

and Palestine. Henceforth, The Great Unknown

next message: Goodbye, Paul McCartney
message deleted. Next message: Hi *message*
deleted. Next message: Looks like we're
playing phone tag here. Well, at the risk
of leaving another embarrassingly long message,
here goes. I had a really good time with you
the other night and I don't want to play games.
I know that I am supposed to wait three days
or five days or whatever society tells us
is the appropriate amount of time, but listen,
I want it to happen again. It was magical.
I'm not ashamed and I hope you aren't either.
I realize expectations are sometimes different
for men and women but I do know this:
it can be really beautiful if two people are
looking for the same thing at the same time,
even if it feels confusing in the morning. I'm tired
of waiting around for the right person! You know?
I don't mean it *that* way. I definitely think you are
the right person for me, or I am interested

in finding out if you are and I really think
that night proves we should give this thing
a chance…I'm just hoping that you are
feeling the way I am feeling about it…
I guess I'm saying I'm willing to take a chance
on *us*, I hope you are *message deleted*.
Next message: I think I got cut off
and I'll make this short and sweet
message deleted. Nevertheless,
brainstems are the missing link? Evolution
believes in particles, quanta, the invisibles—
Underlying causes include: dehydration,
exhaustion, chemical imbalance, diabetes,
hypertension, hypothermia, gout, congestive
heart failure, gangrene, and brainstorming.
And some deep kissing, shocking PDA,
and possibly illegal activity! Clues
explain everything. Index L: T-Rex,
stegosaurus, triceratops, archaeopteryx,
diplodocus, brachiosaurus, iguanodon,

the pterodactyl, the ichthyosaur,

velociraptor, plesiosaur, and trilobite.

When the calls came in. The best of the best

of grisly death and doom and gloom

or vampires and sex? Gothic architecture

is extremely important and flexible

like yogis, or yoginis. Consider egrets

or spy satellites or the dead detective.

Agents are everywhere. Next message:

Hey! What's goin' on! *Message deleted.*

Next message: I know you hear me

message deleted. Next message:

So, you're the asshole? What?!

Message deleted. And furthermore, no,

I am not interested in subscribing. Period.

functions, equivalencies, measurements

parchment paper, papyrus. When everyone

burns in The Purification, salvation

and subtlety, nuance, double entendre,

some stroking, caressing, moaning

and overtly inappropriate licking. Yes,

vermin are everywhere: rapists, murderers,

pedophiles, slavers, child pornographers.

This book is dedicated to my daughter

and televangelists and Disney princesses—

The catchphrase? You can't win the mall.

I should have been a player, shared my gifts—

This book is dedicated to my wife,

and goodbye, Neal Diamond. I'm sorry.

This book is dedicated to my grandfathers

and to courage in the face of insurmountable—

And her letter said: 'Follow your heart, Matt,

in what you want to do. That's what

your grandfather wanted for you.'

Or her letter: 'I haven't been feeling well

lately. I've had a bout with the shingles

and it is a little lonely here, now.

I've included an envelope so you can tell me

all about what you're doing at school."

This book is dedicated to my grandmothers

Index L: I'd like to thank my producer

and my agent who has been with me

through thick and thin and my parents

who have loved me despite my behavior

and public escapades and my fellow actors

and the writers—the writers, the writers!—

for such an amazing script and, of course,

my director. And the janitors and all those

people who put in all those hours making sure

we were taken care of; the makeup people,

the cooks, and of course, my lovely family!

You guys support me going away and leaving

you for long periods of time all because

of this: art and beauty and love and love

and love! I love you all! Thank you!

and toiling away in obscurity? Poetry

or the beaver, in early spring. Consider

the possum, its sickly whiteness, the window

to the soul, or the suburb. Next message:

I've tried calling several *message deleted*

and this book is dedicated to my infant son,
and to explosions, physicality, machinery,
the forces of masculinity. Consider the phallus,
its organizing mythos. Next message:
Listen, this is what I didn't want to happen
message deleted. Next message. Hello again
message deleted. Things to fear: recovery,
failure, wreckage, symptoms, investigations,
squad cars, terrorists, racists, the press,
avalanches, poetic justice, vengeance,
murder, mayhem, bloodshed, gore,
decapitation, industrial contaminants,
the body, the soul, the heart, the mind. No,
I would not like you to use my information.
Next message: This poem is dedicated
to my father *message deleted.* Next message:
message deleted. Goodbye, Paul McCartney.
Next message: *message deleted.* Ergo, this book
is dedicated to my mother. Next message: Love is
message deleted. That was your last message

CODA: THE NEW YOU

apparently this is legal, at the Super 8.

O, my God! Imagine the Super Bowl

without instant replay! Then, the slime ball

referenced *America's Next Top Model*,

and leads, clues and detectives. The internet

monitors, hidden cameras, really rough sex

to leave something for posterity. So they signed

the contract. Pigeons, starlings, cowbirds—

Yes, Christina Aguilera and C-Lo oversee

grisly death, bloated bodies. Archetypes

may refill on sugary drinks, effervescence,

and showmanship. And terrorists, rapists,

murderers, hate crimes, and ethnic cleansing.

Yes, fantasies may be cropped for optimization

or airbrushed, enhanced by latex, fishnet

stockings, soundtracks, strobe lights, or

synchronized choreographies. Capitalism is

the new slavery? Desire is everywhere!

How to make them talk? We have methods.

I saw him then: Justin Bieber.

flavors of the month? Imaginary histories
provide imaginary urgencies, in the interests
of armed conflict. Back at the homestead,
groundbreaking, ribbon cutting, backslapping.
Boys will be boys! Profiling may become
the new you. I saw him then: David Beckham!
when this breadbasket is a plantation! Who,
Taylor Swift? Poetry may become viral,
like species, extinctions, special deliveries
public executions, three-day-old-sweat,
ringleaders, and bankrolled lobbyists. Consider
purchasing ad space, or producing a fantasy:
the weathergirl, her magenta scarf and lip gloss
or violence on the highway, the violence of
another angry white man. In suburbia,
who is next in line? Vengeance, stabbings,
hit-and-runs, school shooters, domestic terrorists,
bullying (online or in person), suicide bombers,
airplane hijackers, surface-to-air missiles,
hostage crises, new kinds of surveillance

call that clickbait? Or you may be presumed

incompetent, or presumed dangerous,

or presumed guilty, or presumed innocent,

or presumed armed, or presumed Black,

or presumed Muslim, or presumed Latino,

or presumed a terrorist, or presumed combative,

or presumed a threat, or presumed weak,

or presumed promiscuous, or presumed exceptional,

or presumed inferior, or presumed to be

Dontre Hamilton or Eric Garner or John Crawford III

or Michael Brown or Ezell Ford or Dante Parker

or Tanisha Anderson or Jerame Reid

or Tony Robinson or Phillip White

or Eric Harris or Walter Scott

or Freddie Gray or Sandra Bland.

Or you may be presumed to be Laquan McDonald

or Trayvon Martin or Oscar Grant

or Rekia Boyd or Shelley Frey or Natasha McKenna.

Or you may be presumed to be Harvey Milk

or Brandon Teena or Matthew Shepherd or

security guards are more humorous
than you might think. For example,
the other day I asked a security guard,
"Why do you stand here all day
like a sleeping cow or long-eared goat
or burbling pigeon or useless emblem?
Whom do you serve?" And he said,
"It's my job, man, now back the fuck off."
LMAO! Just then, the scandalous news
handed it over to the weathergirl and
Sunday, O Sunday! No, unfortunately,
visiting hours can't last forever! Because
you wouldn't preserve their uppermiddleclass
expectations, their preferred social climate.
Control groups may haul bodies into the desert
discreetly, in a flatbed, or dump bodies
into the reservoir from the bridge. Listen,
we have come to expect *real* service,
goddammit! The staff is pleased to announce
the return of the Kardashians to relevance

and corporate welfare, perks, amenities
in the workout room or sauna, the return
of a refurbished star to the Red Carpet
sparkling wine? Because it is a non-contact
sport. That's why. Shepherd or shepherdess?
on to Final Jeopardy. Certain emphases
may initiate prohibitive fantasies: desire
and occasional rainfall are perfectly normal
reactions, as are twitching, spasms, blackouts,
outbursts, sweating, vomiting, dizziness,
lemons, clementines. Who supports the idea
of an intervention? Pan, the goat-footed
heathen, and Bacchus, the long-haired
hipster, and Herman, the weird guy leering—
an exit in the casino? And the condition
of poetry is music, but ambient crap
or loungy stuff, with hangovers and money
to burn. Youth culture is managing the world?
When technology modifies the climate,
gentrification misplaces. Yes, consider

slowly, to the weathergirl. Oh, yes,

I saw him then: George Clooney! Believe

inspirational stories, political statements,

billboards and billionaires, or try an infusion

of lavender bath salts, white tea leaves,

pumice stones, air strikes, blood gushing

everywhere, crumbling buildings, and

children buried in the rubble. Who opposes

the idea? Car crashes and train crashes

and trains crashing into semi trucks

and plane crashes and boat crashes

and boats crashing into water skiers and

SUV's crashing into minimalls, terrific

explosions and Toledo, Dayton, Lima,

Columbus, Cincinnati, Marietta,

Youngstown, Cleveland, Ashtabula,

Geneva, Brecksville, Plain City, Findlay,

Chillicothe, Athens, Oxford, Springfield,

the Ohio River and Lake Erie. Yes, then

I saw him: Jimmy Buffet! The Parrothead!

My work is dedicated to the present

the return of the C-list celebrity from rehab,

chivalry, and the real man's man. See also:

damage control, the race for the cure,

gliomas, carcinomas, sarcomas, and

a warm ray gun? Astronauts at the museum

of unsent love letters? Dear Everyone:

wear something nice to the funeral. Consider

filtering old ideas, conditioned responses,

kneejerk reactions, buck passing, platitudes

and/or habitual action, and Tradition. Yes,

mine fields, chemical weapons from old wars,

mass graves, execution sites, and refugees,

orphaned children or what people do

when they are not being watched. See also:

torturing, raping, spying, detaining. Absolute

certainty? Trust building exercises, share time,

cafeteria meet-and-greets, group activities

in the community room, walking the grounds,

or smooching on the Ferris Wheel! Man,

those kids sure can sing! And dance! Racism

is not normal. The eyes may be trained
on High, or may pass through
the life cycle, blown rocketward. From
Reaganomics to Occupy Wall Street, the hole
in the ozone may damage self-esteem.
Consider fire-retardant space suits,
deregulation, metaphysical love, or the art
of hand grenades: approximation. Or spelunking,
rock climbing, and Ironman competitions
may locate harmful radiation in sperm
whales, gray whales, blue whales,
beluga whales, humpback whales,
whale sharks, even. Orcas. Darwinism
is what it is. Among the varieties of sparrow,
gasoline and carburetors and the power
running game. Yesteryear is always more
convincing. For example, fleshing out
your fantasy may require workshopping
or the male gaze may disrobe more slyly;
everything is relative. Have you heard

the one about the invisible man? Consider

the occasional disfiguring acid burn, kidnapping,

or ritual mutilation. Modern warfare involves

explicit interpretations of BP and Texaco,

as well as talking heads, infomercials,

investment portfolios, and back-scratching.

Inner peace can be really expensive. Yes,

one basic premise may clog up the machinery;

locating the right artery is more important

than youth culture? Machine guns, tanks,

AR-15s, and rocket launchers. Perhaps

they should demonstrate the position? Hey,

that is your problem, my friend! Now that

God is dead and Michael Jackson is dead

and Whitney Houston and Prince are also dead.

I wear dark glasses when thinking of you

in holding cells or maximum security prisons—

Yes, certain fantasies may trigger

feelings of enhanced masculinity; how they

idolize killing and believe in divine justice

for example. When the graphic body
suffered devastating losses. The 7-day forecast
eliminated the possibility of an alibi. Yes,
escape clauses may redeem humanity, but
mannequins may be standoffish. Models
are templates we can believe in! Now we are
all on the same page! On a scale of 1–10…
So, burning sensations? Painful urination?
the spirit of innovation! On Facebook,
Pasiphae complained to the local authorities.
or Rihanna? Or Katy Perry? Or Lady Gaga?
Someone who can really belt out
the national anthem. Certain anathema
are invigorating. Demagogues instill
reactions. There is too much to memorize!
receive apologies or give thanks
to the advisory board. So, I pressed
the button. Kaboom! Seriously? Yes,
under the new regime, objective truth
is somewhat shapeable. You feel me?

and calendars, afternoon radio, argyle socks,

ashtrays, hard candies, flower prints,

potpourri, pinball machines, jukeboxes,

figurines, and cuckoo clocks. Demonstrate

the position in public?! And furthermore,

can the room be arranged as we like?

bedsores, bedpans, IVs, heart monitors

and petunias, violets, impatiens, daisies,

verbena, hydrangea, soothing piano music,

cadavers, the morgue, ID placards. Peace

is the result of the executive function

of the brain; physical science, military science,

and war as history, or the history of great battles,

valor, invincible heroes, and heroic defeats.

Certain neurological disorders may intensify

the winds of change. To produce

bravado, offer the halos of yesteryear.

I saw him then: Peyton Manning. And/or

Tiger Woods! Consider kinship ties

and wedding vows. The Surgeon General

how they despise The Leader and also
The People. Beware: exchange rates,
inoculations, passports, marching bands,
and majorettes at halftime. Old ideas
mean everything exclusionary. For instance,
were I an aftershave model, or spokesperson
for almanacs or encyclopedias? Viagra,
Rohypnol, Xanax, Celexa, Effexor, or Lithium
might suggest deliverable policies,
a grand old debauch, a BBQ, tailgating,
beer pong, body paint, and streaking
(for college football games only! Rah!).
Yes, corroborators are stranding bytes—
which roadside? With new mythologies,
the Roy Rogers? At the trucker's mall?
are the beds *that* comfortable? Anomalies
are necessary, as well as transfusions,
preventative treatments, preemptive strikes,
ordering, filing, labeling, targeting, profiling,
and providing palliative care. For instance,

trauma. I listen to the birds every morning
and am terribly savage in my criticism
of television programs, corporations, memes
and most forms of authority, but silently,
like magic. I am as complacent as the next guy
but will respond to your emails and texts
in days, or sometimes weeks, or months,
but faithfully, depending on the weather
up there and the whirling satellites.
I definitely like your activities, hobbies,
and pics of happy children, your detailed
music and movie selections, your status
updates and whimsical asides, but I am also
passionate about destroying dominant
history, narratives, and reification, and distrust
the trend of fashioning an idealized image
of who I want you to think I think I am, and
having that simulation embody me. Of course,
visit me at my homepage and I will leave
the nightlight on, the bed turned down

and learn the hard way. Self-promotion
is absolutely essential; as a coronary
I would like to suggest, with respect to
the return of springtime, the Korai,
Demeter, a light rain, cherry blossoms,
calligraphy, poetry, and cheeping,
which, roughly translated, means:
"Feed me!" "Feed me!" "Feed me!"
Consider the new ways America packages
the myths it lives on, like meritocracy,
the inherent goodness of hard work,
the preservation of body and self image,
or competition presided over by privilege.
Yes, were I a singer/songwriter I would
begin with "Blackbird," like everyone,
or possibly "American Pie." Ergo,
pelicans, sandpipers, seagulls, albatrosses,
dolphin pods, little sand crabs, conchs, and
technological evolution. Because of these
flashes of absolute rage, I scare myself

and wait up for the weathergirl. Suppose
the power goes out, after hours, or all
these machines malfunction? Who would
come to save me? Or suppose I am left here
to inhabit this silence within me; all visitors
turned away, the bustle of the day, still;
these doors permanently sealed? Or suppose
I enter this narrative the way I departed
the other: suppose I am the falling body
that never returned from the panorama
but dispersed into it; that they will lift
this broken text into their hearts,
and that it will wrench us all out of time? Or,
suppose that I have now become a cipher,
that their voices compose me, suffering
composes me; that in its immensity—
Yes, I maintain a dream journal, but
sometimes there is no escape. When
at a potluck, bring something! Sure,
install a surveillance camera! An alarmed

sociopath is more dangerous. Coordinates
will do, in a pinch. Although mythology
and psychology may contribute to the damage
report, the weather is absolutely perfect
here, and sleep will come. Yes, the weather
is beautiful here, where the shimmering being
has come for me, and lifted me away, away—
stalkers, sex traffickers, child pornographers
attend the farmer's markets and playgrounds.
Pedophiles practice mimicry, and may believe
in homegrown remedies. The art of persuasion
arises in humble urges and good-natured
ribbing. I am a silver spoon, and language
slips beyond good and evil, like technology.
Consider Andromeda, chained, or
I saw him then: Derek Jeter, Mr. Yankee!
and redness, splotchiness, blotching, rashes,
goiters, hives, ulcers, eczema, discharges—
because terrorism is never unique, one may
drink at the fountain of Deliverance. Belong

to a club, or damage others. The End

requested a timeout? Praise uplifts!

because of the rural poor and the urban poor,

capitalism may experience white guilt

or retaliatory bravado. Media sensationalism

and classism because American; they became

the ones who stayed behind, telling stories

about the way things used to be, goddammit. Are

overnight accommodations needed? Furthermore,

Europa complained to the local authorities.

Ganymede complained to the local authorities.

and green screens, acetate, the dark rooms

of the soul, the importance of the natural

metaphor as substitute for any real emotion.

Consider the rain and wind and sun and clouds,

this lovely weather, and these projections

of the weathergirl; transmissions from

The Great Beyond! Out on the highway

of the past, the patrolman soliloquizes:

"Hark wanderers. We shall overcome

uncertainty and doubt. Take it and eat. Or,

imagine that you are a Stratocaster

and I am strumming you at an increasingly

violent pace. This is precisely how I feel;

I am precise. Love means everything

when in the crosshairs. Killing may occur

in the woods with high-powered sniper rifles,

deer blinds, camouflage, and inalienable rights.

Or, once, the crystalline sky quenched

my desire for a soul, and I was the soul

of the world, and world was pure soul:

ATMAN. Yes, Ahimsa.

Or, I was a clotted nightmare, burst infection,

or fractured lullaby. Were you a grenade,

I would toss you into almost any schematic,

or control group. Because of hatred,

violent encounters at the bus stop or hotel

or interesting websites. Safe Search is OFF.

Torture devices are available, and local women—

At the stroke of midnight, the princess flees

the music of the spheres? Interpreters
are standing by their reasons. Warning: I am
your revisionary poiesis, a resistant strain—
you want filmic illusions? I saw him then:
Jonathan Franzen! Deliberately, the maniac
reloaded. Deliberately, the maniac reloaded.
Reloaded. Outside the gates, select barbarians
will be provided backstage passes. Consider
the inoperable tumor, the slow growth
of the unidentified mass. I am that biopsy.
I cannot be beautiful; I am beauty itself—
and the rain, the wind, the clouds, the sun,
knights in shimmering ardor. Make amends—
mysticism is more useful than overproduction,
or the rabbit's foot, dragon, and sorcery.
Then, the Romantic Poets returned
and set up Facebook and Twitter accounts
and friended everyone, and when we saw
the silly things that they thought and did
in their off hours, we formed a phalanx

and offered glad tidings. The landscape
is death itself. I am a house in the mouth
of death, by the roadside of death
reading the poetry of death. And gladioli,
gardenias, morning glories, climbing vines
of all sorts, gardening manuals, pruning
shears, protective eyewear, gloves, a spray
of daisies, and lots of verbena and bees.
As for the weathergirl: gaze on.
Imagine that you are the protagonist
of a video game, or that you have moved
past attachment, intimacy, and politics.
Out on the highway of the past,
may you roam free or die trying. Behold:
the new togetherness awaits. Dear Everyone:
I want to create and to create a world with you
in these brief instants of our shared lives;
may The Rapture remain incomplete.
No, do not believe the agents.
Do not believe the agendas.

Do not believe the official story.

Do not believe the preachers.

Do not believe the media moguls.

Do not believe the life coaches.

Do not believe the advocates.

Do not believe the believers.

Do not believe the truth we tell ourselves.

Do not believe the afternoon talk show.

Do not believe the strip malls.

Do not believe the poets.

Do not believe the spokespersons.

Do not believe the advisors.

Do not believe the administration.

Do not believe the strategic plan.

Do not believe the letter from the CEO.

Do not believe the experts.

Do not believe public opinion.

Do not believe litanies, or

terms & conditions, or some restrictions

may apply. Consider the universe

and how all human projects fail. Yes,

what we need now is a paper pusher,

someone who is detail-oriented, task-driven,

more or less humorous during happy hour,

not terribly ambitious, utterly expendable

but endocrine disruptors are everywhere!

as well as China, Malaysia, Singapore,

Thailand, Laos, Cambodia, Vietnam,

Outer Mongolia, Inner Mongolia,

both Koreas, and Japan. The amnesty

is false. The security commission is false.

The regulatory committee is false. The CIA

is false. The NSA is false. The FBI

is false. The DHS is false. Watchdogs

may have lolling tongues. According to

the media, urgency may be the root

of the rise of demonization. One might

enter into sex rings by rubbing, stroking

licking, petting, or playfully nibbling

martyrs, zealots insurgents, rebels

blessed are the meek; they shall be

driven out; blessed are the just;

they shall be held accountable; blessed

are the empathetic; they shall be shamed;

blessed are the peaceful; they shall be

condemned; and he who orchestrates

the military occupation or strategic

plan shall inherit the spoils. I am so viral!

Furthermore, the Philadelphia 76ers

or Boston Celtics? Yes, believe in

a better world. I saw him then: Carson Daly!

and eclogues, verdant springy steps,

sunny porticoes, fountains; idylls

are beyond the scope of cosmology,

freedom and chance. Despite this,

dermatology, herpetology, rickets, boils,

and foreclosure scenarios. Consider

the cartoon animal, its natural habitat.

The envelope please. And the winner is…

silicon, or insincerity, hypocrisy, cant

or flesh, blood, ash, dust, and prophecy

this book is dedicated to racism, sexism,
imperialism, colonialism, hatred, violence,
ethnic cleansing, the military-industrial
complex, systemic inequities, and also lying.
Any imparted knowledge or conscience is
brought to you by programmed robots. Now
that science fiction is redundant, beware
the contiguous physicality of remembrance,
as well as projection models, flow charts,
statistical anomalies and buzzwords. Yes,
because your body is your body; her body
is her body; his body is his body; because
their bodies are their bodies; because
our bodies are our bodies. This book is
dedicated to all other victims, to silence,
forgetfulness, unforgivable truths, destroyed
histories, ongoing deaths-in-life: patriarchy.
Consider the lapping of the infinite sea
within your mind, the nadis of your third eye,
an eternally rising sun within you: perfect, pure

untouched. Partly cloudy with a 10% chance—

childhood sleeps in love. Are you LinkedIn?

insurance salesmen may require more data. Yes,

believe the authority of facts, the reign

of causation. Regarding genetically modified

ideas, suspicions, conspiracies, surveillance,

and green living: I am ecofriendly,

a citizen of the world, and cannot understand

permanent war, the production of new enemies,

the return of fundamentalism, of essentialism

of the B-list celebrity from rehab, of reality

television. One must become an activist

in the Golden Age of Violence. Always

be closing something down. See also:

Google, Yahoo, Amazon, Apple. Yes,

they enforce new conformities, and shape

subjectivity in the name of Freedom—

So the Achaeans set sail. So the Trojans set sail.

So the Argonauts set sail. So the missiles fly.

When in doubt, survive the onslaught

and they are reading my email.

And they are sifting through my texts.

And they are recording my conversations.

And they are stealing my information.

And they are encrypting my desires.

And they are programming my consciousness.

And they are waiting for me in an unmarked car.

And they are leveling my past.

And they are capitalizing on my present.

And they are turning me into an algorithm.

And they are targeting my children.

And they are victimizing the poor.

And they are murdering in my name.

And they are pillaging in my name.

And they are nation-building in my name.

And they are extending empire in my name.

And they are watching me in the surveillance camera.

And they are typing this poem on my computer.

And they have brought me here, to this nice, warm place

where they, they too, are hard at work, on the new you—

Matt Shears is the author of *10,000 Wallpapers* (Brooklyn Arts Press 2011) and *Where a road had been* (BlazeVox 2010). He was a Schaefer Fellow at the University of Nevada Las-Vegas, and is a graduate of the Iowa Writers Workshop. He has taught most recently at California College of the Arts in Oakland and San Francisco, and at the San Francisco Art Institute. He lives in Berkeley, California with his family.

More Literary Titles
from the
Brooklyn Arts Press
Catalogue

All books are available at BrooklynArtsPress.com

MNSID
NEW

63768442R00124